CITY *of* PRAYER

Transform Your Community through Praying Churches

Trey Kent and Kie Bowman

Terre Haute, IN

PrayerShop Publishing is the publishing arm of the Church Prayer Leaders Network. The Church Prayer Leaders Network exists to equip and inspire local churches and their prayer leaders in their desire to disciple their people in prayer and to become a "house of prayer for all nations." Its online store, prayershop.org, has more than 150 prayer resources available for purchase or download.

ISBN (Print): 978-1-935012-88-7
ISBN: (E-Book): 978-1-935012-89-4

1 2 3 4 5 | 2023 2022 2021 2020 2019

DEDICATION

I dedicate this book to Joann and Dan Davis. No one has made a greater impact on the spiritual climate of our city than you two. We all stand on your shoulders. We are a city of prayer because you pioneered the way. I honor you and love you.

Trey Kent
AUSTIN, TEXAS

I dedicate this work to Shirley and Joe Hayman, who worked tirelessly for years at Hyde Park Baptist Church to build one of the finest church prayer ministries I have ever seen. Their hearts burn with passion for the Lord and for prayer. I love them dearly.

Kie Bowman
AUSTIN, TEXAS

ACKNOWLEDGMENTS

We have a lot of people to thank for this book. The concept for writing our story was first suggested by Ronnie Floyd, who is a national leader in the prayer movement and believes in our ministry of prayer in Austin, Texas. We are deeply grateful to Dr. Floyd for his vision for this book, seeing its potential value to other cities and leaders, his encouragement to write it, and his help getting us connected with the publisher. Without him, this book would not have happened.

We are also indebted to Jonathan Graf and the team at PrayerShop Publishing. They are a pleasure to work with, and we appreciate the grace extended to us as the first deadline came and went! We hope it is worth the wait. We look forward to the possibility of other projects with them in the future.

We also feel a deep sense of comradery with the other members of the Unceasing Prayer Movement team. Will Davis Jr., N. Jordan Mkwanazi, Abraham Perez, Rick Randall, and David Smith have been a part of every step along the way. Not only did they help us conceptualize the outline and framework of the book, but they have lived the Unceasing Prayer Movement story. We cannot imagine this ministry without this team.

When the opportunity for this book first came our way, we met with the entire Unceasing Prayer Movement team and talked through the structure of the book and how two authors would write one story. As a team, we discussed each of our strengths and unique perspectives. The two of us outlined the book and determined who would write which chapters. Along the way we made some adjustments to the original plan, but we always agreed to write our own, independent chapters. Then we wove the chapters into final form by reading and contributing comments on each other's chapters. Still, the chapters identified with one name are the work of that author alone.

In addition to the writing of the book, considerable effort goes into the editorial process. We wish to thank Mary Anne Kent and Becky Shipp for their invaluable insights as they read, edited, and made suggestions about the manuscript prior to sending it to the publisher. Any mistakes or errors are naturally our own, but without the help of these two women, the final manuscript would not be complete.

We also wish to thank the many authors, thought leaders, and prayer pioneers who have guided our thoughts through the years leading up to the writing of this book. We have attempted to acknowledge sources wherever appropriate, but our own interest in the subject and ministry of prayer has been influenced by so many people. Undoubtedly, their thoughts have become almost unconsciously embedded in our own thoughts. This work is original but has been informed by the work of so many who have come before us. Wherever our thoughts, expressions, or vocabulary reflect the writings of others and have not been cited, we can only say it is unconscious on our part due to the heavy influence of previous thinkers on the significant subject of prayer.

Both of us are pastors of local churches, so we must thank our congregations for being a part of the prayer movement and for allowing the time we needed to complete this manuscript. No two pastors could be any more grateful for the churches they serve. Thank you to Northwest Fellowship and Hyde Park Baptist/The Quarries Church for your vision and passion for the prayer movement in our city and beyond.

Finally, we must thank our wives and partners in ministry, Mary Anne Kent and Tina Bowman. These two Christian women help us do what God calls us to do and offer patient encouragement as we labor in the prayer movement—and even when we worked strange hours to finish this book.

Trey Kent
Kie Bowman
Austin, Texas

TABLE OF CONTENTS

FOREWORD

Seeds of another great spiritual awakening are being planted in cities across our nation, and they are especially starting to bud in places like Austin, Texas; Bellingham, Washington; and in scores of churches across New Mexico—and beyond. Having watched and participated in prayer movements and strategies here and abroad over the past five decades, there is something about this movement that fills my heart with hopeful anticipation that a tipping point for true revival and awakening in our nation, and even worldwide, is on the horizon. The book you hold in your hands provides powerful evidence that this is much more than just another program to be added to already-packed local church calendars. Trey Kent and Kie Bowman, pastors in Austin, Texas, have experienced it in dramatic ways. They document the fruit of this growing movement in this timely book *City of Prayer.*

City of Prayer begins by describing how Holy Spirit-inspired prayer movements of the past gave birth to revivals that impacted the entire world and led to some of the greatest advances of the gospel in history. The authors go on to explain how the same is happening today, but indicators are the global Church in this present hour may be on the threshold of something the Church has never seen. At the heart of this is a uniting of churches of all denominations in saturating their communities with day and night, 24/7 prayer, led and inspired by pastoral leadership at a local church level.

Authors Kent and Bowman also clearly convey that God's strategy for advancing the gospel and building His Church always has had its roots in prayer. The first-century Church was first and foremost a praying Church. The Book of Acts is one of the greatest books on prayer ever written. Kent and Bowman point out that the current emerging citywide prayer movement in their community is far from being an anomaly of the 21st century, but it's a prayer movement that is a recovery of the original first-century purpose of God. I couldn't agree more.

What especially encourages me is how this movement—basically built around local churches each taking a day a month to sustain 24/7 prayer—does even more than the impact of the prayer itself on any given day. It ultimately creates a growing culture of prayer in all the participating churches of the community. True, some larger congregations could mobilize their members to sustain 24/7 prayer—and some have. But when many churches join together, with each taking their share in the citywide movement, a supernatural unity begins to take shape. It is like Acts 4:31–32: "And when they had prayed . . . the multitude of those who believed were of one heart and one soul. . ." (NKJV).

The authors also highlight how prayer movements fueled the great awakenings of the past, such as the nation-changing revival of 1857–1858. That awakening was born out of a humble, noon prayer meeting with a handful of businessmen. Before long thousands were praying daily up and down the East Coast of America. At one point in the revival conversions reached 50,000 a week, a number that I understand continued for at least two full years. Kent and Bowman build a strong case for "Why not today? Why not in your city? Why not in America—and even the whole world?"

Thankfully, this book doesn't end with merely a look at what God has done through prayer in past generations. In addition, they provide practical insight from years of seeing this movement grow in their own city. Praying God's promises in a unified way among all participating churches is but one example. The authors also show how this movement has given birth to a sweeping and multiplying strategy (called America Prays) now being implemented by major denominations and ministerial community alliances across the landscape of our nation. Brian Alarid, who heads up America Prays, is a New Mexico pastor who has seen multiple churches in communities across his state unite in sustained day-and-night prayer. Together with Jason Hubbard, a pastor in Bellingham, Washington, who helped pioneer this citywide prayer strategy, Alarid, Kent, and Bowman are being used of the Lord to trumpet this vision across America and even to nations beyond. Already in cities where this simple but impactful strategy is implemented, greater unity in the Body of Christ is demonstrated, resulting in increased racial fellowship and reconciliation. Kent and Bowman have certainly seen it happen in Austin, Texas. They provide encouraging documentation in the pages that follow, including inspiring testimonies from eyewitnesses.

City of Prayer could well be a spark to ignite a firestorm of prayer, the likes of which our nation has never seen. The local church is the kindling, waiting and ready. Together, let's help fan the flames!

Dick Eastman
International President, Every Home for Christ
President of America's National Prayer Committee

Chapter One

PRAYING FOR YOUR CITY

By Kie Bowman

Jim Cymbala walked out of my office with a determined stride, headed to our church's worship center. He was accompanied by a vice president from the Billy Graham Evangelistic Association who had come to Austin, Texas, intent on visiting privately with the Brooklyn pastor.

They were busy in a conversation, so I motioned the direction we were headed and fell in a few steps behind them. As we entered the worship center of Hyde Park Baptist Church, the room was filling up with 2,000 people from around the city, chattering with excitement about the prayer gathering about to begin.

It was only nine years earlier when pastor Trey Kent stood unceremoniously under a light pole at midnight in his neighborhood, praying with his wife Mary Anne, and sensing the leadership of God concerning prayer for the city. Clearly, the packed room and the excitement about prayer was evidence that God had a plan for Trey, for Austin, and for the ministry of day-and-night prayer.

That gathering wasn't the only evidence that God is using prayer to unify the Body of Christ and raise the spiritual temperature in Austin. It was only one of the more recent; there have been many others. That's partially what this book is about.

We intend to clearly document the exciting story of how one pastor's citywide, God-sized vision started a spiritual chain reaction for unceasing prayer that is currently altering the Kingdom culture of one of America's largest and fastest-growing cities. It's an exciting and well-documented story.

More than merely telling our story, however, this book will serve as a strategic guide for other visionary leaders, prayer warriors, and city transformers who sense a call to launch or fuel an unceasing prayer movement in their cities. As you read, ask yourself one question: *Is God calling me to lead my city in unceasing prayer?*

EPICENTER CITIES

Where do you think revival and spiritual awakening are most likely to occur? A move of God that transforms churches and impacts culture is most likely to touch down in the most unlikely place, since that's the place it's most likely needed. To be more specific, if a city looks too far gone or a culture seems too distant from God for an awakening, you may be surprised. God shows up in hard places precisely because they're hard. Every culture far from Him is deeply in need of Him. In the same way that light shines brightest in the darkest rooms, God reveals His glory in the most unlikely places.

Those who have studied or remember the Jesus Movement in the 1970s will agree that spiritual awakening on a national scale seemed wildly unlikely among America's disillusioned youth culture, until it happened and changed a generation and the trajectory of an entire culture. I saw it happen in my hometown. It was like spontaneous combustion. One minute, Christianity was on the fringes of the city. The next minute, former dope-smoking hippies and counterculture youth were witnessing for Jesus in the halls of our high schools and on the streets of our city.

For years I wondered how it had happened. What caused it? We were a long way from the beaches of Southern California or the chapel services of a Methodist college in Kentucky where the movement erupted. We were a largely unchurched city with few evangelicals. Years after the Jesus Movement, I met a family who knew part of the story.

Prayer played a role.

A few years ago, a woman I had never met and her husband attended a church in Tennessee where I was preaching at an evangelistic meeting. They waited to see me after the service. In the 1960s, she had also lived in my hometown of Fairbanks, Alaska. She told me her father had been pastor of a small church. When I learned which church, I was momentarily confused because she named one of the largest churches in town. As she told her story, it became clear. Her father had been pastor of a small church, but it got big because it was the epicenter of the Jesus Movement.

The small-church pastor struggled for years to reach people, but nothing worked. So he and a little group started to pray about a way to make a difference in their unchurched city. The pastor decided to step out in faith and invite a team from David Wilkerson's Teen Challenge to lead a revival emphasis. For months he led his church to persist in prayer for a move of God. A few weeks before Teen Challenge arrived, the pastor became ill—and he and his family were transferred to a warmer climate in a southern state. They didn't learn until much later that more than 100 teenagers and young adults were saved through the Wilkerson crusade. During the Jesus Movement, that church was the one where most of the "Jesus freaks" attended.

As the pastor's daughter related her side of the story and I connected it to the side I knew, we stood in a Tennessee church lobby and realized her father's prayers and efforts had ignited the Jesus Movement in an unlikely place! The pastor never realized his desperate prayers lit a fuse that exploded into a spiritual awakening. That's how God works. He responds to prayer. And He can do it again. Does that pastor's desperate prayer and step of faith encourage you to pray and step out in faith for your city? What's stopping you?

Today there are prayer movements growing in the most unlikely places. In a later chapter, we will describe the prayer movement in Bellingham, Washington, where the city of almost 90,000 people is covered in day-and-night prayer. We will mention the surprising work of God emerging because of prayer in the otherwise spiritually indifferent city of Reno, Nevada. Recently, a prayer movement with a nationwide vision has come to life in Albuquerque, New Mexico. Of course, we also want to tell you about what God is doing in one of our state's most unchurched cities—our own city—Austin, Texas. I believe these are *epicenter cities*. Allow me to explain.

As previously mentioned, I am from Fairbanks, Alaska. In Alaska, we are familiar with earthquakes. In fact, the largest earthquake ever recorded in America occurred in Anchorage in 1964. Actually, of the top 20 worst earthquakes recorded in the United States, 13 of them have been in Alaska.[1] I've lived through serious earthquakes and minor tremors. When an earthquake hits, the rumbling can be felt in a radius reaching out across hundreds of miles. But there is always an epicenter. The epicenter is the location immediately above where the quake originates and is usually the place where the magnitude is greatest.

Revival is like an earthquake. It seems to suddenly shake us into a greater awareness of God's presence. The rumbling power is felt in an area wider than its center. There are factors leading to revival, just as there are unseen factors leading to physical earthquakes.

SOMETHING IS COMING

Today, the tectonic plates of culture are shifting beneath our feet. We are so familiar with the major changes occurring in American culture that it's almost unnecessary to list the moral decline, the hostility and polarization in our political process, the spike in the depression and suicide rates among teens and children, the opioid crisis, racial divisions, and the growth of atheism and secularism. Unfortunately, the list goes on. In many ways, the country isn't changing—it *has* changed. No one knows where it will stop. Change itself isn't bad, but change in the direction of godlessness is deadly.

Fortunately, God is active, and the Church is sensing a desperation that leads to prayer. There is a prayer movement rising with the potential to usher in the most widespread spiritual awakening in American history. Perhaps the most significant event since Pentecost is on the way. Some days I feel certain that's the case. Why? *I believe God hears and answers prayer.*

Across the nation God is raising up individual prayer ministries, movements, pastors, churches, and leaders in strange, unlikely places. These may be epicenters of a coming revival ushered in by the most unified prayer movement in American history. Actually, it seems to be global. God is moving everywhere through a swelling prayer movement which points to something on the horizon sent from heaven, the likes of which we've never seen before.

Are you called to this movement? Are you burdened to see more people come to Christ, the Church unified, and "times of refreshing . . . from the presence of the Lord" (Acts 3:20)? If your city isn't praying together like this, perhaps you're the one who will go on the "walls" of your city like a watchman in prayer and start fulfilling the ancient prophecy: "On your walls, O Jerusalem, I have set watchmen; all the day and all the night they shall never be silent. You who put the Lord in remembrance, take no rest, and give him no rest until he establishes Jerusalem and makes it a praise in the earth" (Isa. 62:6–7).

Something is coming, and the prayer movement is the harbinger. Barely ten years ago, Trey Kent, a pastor who was plenty busy leading his own church, sensed God calling him to unify other pastors across the rapidly growing city of Austin, Texas, to cover the city in day-and-night prayer. It seemed like an overwhelming task, but today hundreds of believers from churches of all kinds cover our city in prayer 24 hours a day, seven days a week, 365 days a year. The results have been astonishing, and we believe we're just getting started.

I'm certain, based on what I've seen, that someone reading these words right now is burning with passion to lead a movement in his or her city, too. Prayer is like fire—it ignites everything it touches and continues spreading. Revival and spiritual awakening are like an earthquake that shifts and shakes the culture because of unceasing, desperate prayer. The days of *business as usual* for the Church are gone. It's time to pray as the early Church prayed and expect our cities to be epicenters of awakening! "And when they had prayed, the place in which they were gathered together was shaken, and they were all filled with the Holy Spirit and continued to speak the word of God with boldness" (Acts 4:31).

Only one question remains about this kind of relentless prayer: *Is it biblical?* That's essentially the same question Trey Kent wondered when he sensed God calling him to lead a citywide movement. God reminded him of 1 Thessalonians 5:17, which commands the Body of Christ to "pray without ceasing." In the next chapter, we'll explore whether this model of unceasing prayer is an anomaly of modern times or a return to biblical Christianity. Whatever the answer, it should be clear from Scripture.

CHAPTER TWO

PRAYER: THE NEW TESTAMENT MODEL

By Kie Bowman

A church leader meant well when he approached me after a Sunday morning service to advise me that he didn't agree with me. The New Testament Church, he had concluded, was not to be built around the model of a house of prayer. After that brief conversation, I returned to the New Testament with one question in mind: If we are to build houses of prayer, wouldn't the actions and practice of the early Church help us decide? After all, if prayer is the foundation for ministry, it should be clear in Scripture.

In other words, was the early Church a praying Church?

WHY PRAYER?

Before we explore the practical disciplines and components common in prayer movements, we should answer a basic question: *Why should any of us prioritize prayer?* There can be only one compelling reason why we continually urge the Church to pray and why we devote so much time and energy to mobilizing prayer in our churches and in our city: prayer is the New Testament model for ministry.

If persistent prayer is essential for ministry today, we should be able to demonstrate that prayer was essential to Jesus, His apostles, and the early Church. In other words, if Scripture teaches the Lord viewed and practiced prayer as the bedrock discipline for His ministry, it should be easy enough to trace that truth. Once we see it demonstrated biblically, most Christians will agree prayer must undergird all our ministries today as well. After all, for most believers, the Bible guides our faith and practice. So, what does the New Testament teach us about prayer?

ROLE MODELS IN PRAYER

Our best role models are found in the pages of Scripture. Let's consider three biblical role models for prayer. By reviewing these biblical examples, we will see that prayer was God's plan for advancing His Kingdom 2,000 ago—and remains so today.

JESUS: OUR EXAMPLE IN PRAYER

Our search for a role model in prayer might easily and powerfully begin and end with Jesus of Nazareth. In the Gospels, there are at least 18 individual examples of Jesus in prayer. As many other writers and communicators have wondered before, I must also ask: *If Jesus needed to pray, what does that suggest about the priority of prayer in my life?* At the very least, shouldn't we model our prayer lives after His?

If we compare the fruitfulness of our ministries to His, we will eventually wonder if the difference between Him and us is the difference between His prayer life and ours. To help us capture the picture of His model for the ministry of prayer and follow that example, let's examine four scenes from the prayer life of Jesus.

1. JESUS: Prayerfully Confronting the Enemy (Matt. 4:1–11). The first three Gospels record Jesus going to the desert to fast and be tempted by the devil before He launched His public ministry. Although the word *prayer* is never mentioned in these familiar passages, it is reasonable and appropriate to assume Jesus spent His time in prayer. In most every reference of the numerous passages throughout both Testaments where fasting is mentioned, it is accompanied by prayer. The two disciplines go hand in hand. It is incomprehensible to think Jesus fasted 40 days without spending almost all that time in prayer.

So, what does the desert experience suggest to us about prayer in our own lives? Candidly, there are numerous lessons learned in Jesus' desert fast, but two are important for this overview.

First, Jesus delved deeply into the spiritual disciplines to personally overcome the onslaught of satanic attack. His experience gives us an excellent example of how to face temptation when we are spiritually oppressed or attacked. We must fast and pray when we are the target of satanic oppression or severe temptation.

Next, it is clear Jesus prioritized prayer as a strategy for ministry. He had just been baptized, signifying the launch of His public ministry. For the next three years, He focused on redeeming the lost world. How did He begin His urgent worldwide rescue mission? He retreated to the solitude of the desert to seek God and defeat the enemy. At the very least, His commitment to time alone with God (almost a month and a half), when His mission was urgently calling, reminds us that time with God is an indispensable part of the mission. Prayer, in other words, takes priority in the lives of those who hope to serve God effectively.

2. JESUS: Finding God's Will in Prayer (Luke 6:12–16). A nationally known and highly effective ministry leader told me recently he is only as good as the people around him. No one, including Jesus, serves God effectively without teaming with other people. When Jesus was ready to call the 12 apostles out from among His larger following of disciples, He spent the entire night in prayer before making His final decision. Prayer should play a role in our decision-making process, too.

The all-night mountain prayer of Jesus reminds us how important prayer is in determining the specific will of God where there is no direct scriptural promise or counsel for our specific situation in life. Jesus believed decisions should be bathed in prayer to sense the prompting of God's Spirit or to hear His voice.

One other thing is obvious in the mountain prayer of Jesus: He devoted plenty of time to the process. This was no quick, perfunctory prayer asking for generic blessings like the prayers we sometimes pray prior to church meetings or in public settings. Instead, Jesus devoted hours to prayer and thus opened His mind and heart to hearing God's voice and following God's leadership in whatever specific direction might please the Lord.

You and I often have big decisions to make, too. And since we do not know the future, we should be eager to know God's will for us. Remember, we don't pray to get our will done in heaven but to get God's will done on earth.

3. JESUS: The Priority of Prayer (Mark 1:35). Monday for pastors is usually the worst day of the week. Some pastors equate them with the feeling of a physical hangover.[2] As a pastor, I know the feeling of the Monday blues. After the exhilaration and challenges of a long Sunday, pastoral emotions can run high on the Lord's Day and easily "bottom out" the next day. On Mondays, I can feel sluggish, emotionally depleted, and at my lowest spiritually. When asked if Monday is their day off, many pastors say "no" because they don't want to feel that bad on their own time! The Monday blues are a real issue for many pastors and ministry leaders.

Why do I mention this? Jesus had Mondays, too. Mark 1:35 is a bellwether passage when studying the prayer life of Jesus, and it so happens, it occurred on the first day of the work week—the equivalent of a modern Monday morning! A review of the passage leading to verse 35 shows Jesus ministering the previous day, virtually all day, on a busy Sabbath. He taught in the synagogue, healed many sick people, and cast out demons throughout the day and into the evening (Mark 1:21–34).

His busy schedule makes verse 35 even more revealing because He got out of bed so early in the morning we might consider it the middle of the night. In fact, the text emphasizes the time in specific, descriptive, meticulously detailed terms: "And rising very early in the morning, while it was still dark . . ."

Two things are worth noting here. First, the time described as "very early in the morning" gives us a clue to the exact time. The phrase itself, which includes the word "morning," translates a technical word referring to the fourth watch of the night, between 3:00 and 6:00 a.m. Then, to add context, Mark tells us it was still dark. The word for dark in this passage is the Greek word *nux* from which we get the English word *nocturnal*, perhaps suggesting it was much closer to 3:00 a.m. than 6:00 a.m.

Everything about this passage describes the determination of Jesus to prioritize prayer in His personal life and ministry. He rose early, even though He was tired. He left the house and sought solitude. In fact, He found a place for prayer reminiscent of His 40 days alone in the desert. The word *desolate* in verse 35, is the same word translated *wilderness* in verse 12. There is no actual wilderness or desert in the lush area around Capernaum in Galilee. Jesus was clearly replicating His desert experience, as nearly as He could, by seeking the most isolated and deserted place possible for prayer. Why? Jesus recognized the value of secret, undisturbed, time alone with God.

Jesus lived in prayer. Personal difficulties and inconveniences failed to dissuade Him from personally and continuously seeking God. His example alone should be all the incentive we need to prioritize prayer, regardless of what troubles or challenges we face in life.

4. JESUS: Praying through Pain (Matt. 26:36–46). Years ago, when one of my daughters was sick and was scheduled for a hospital stay, I felt deeply distressed and emotional at the thought of how it would impact her. My wife and I shed frequent tears throughout the day. That night, I reached my quota of feeling bad. I was numb. Emotions can wear us out!

One of the most emotionally draining moments of Jesus' life occurred the night before He was crucified. In the Garden of Gethsemane, in a large olive grove on the western slope of the Mount of Olives, Jesus prayed, just hours before His death. Before He passionately cried out to God in prayer, He confided to His closest followers, "My soul is very sorrowful, even to death; remain here, and watch with me" (Matt. 26:38). Jesus' sadness was overwhelming. His emotions were so raw He felt as if they would kill Him!

Jesus felt what we sometimes feel—deep, scarring, emotional pain. His solution for that depth of anguish was twofold. He wanted to pray, and He wanted His friends to pray with Him.

We all know the disciples let Him down, but Christ's request for prayer partners teaches us not to face life's tragedies without a prayer team around us.

To summarize, what do we learn about prayer from our ultimate role model? Jesus waged spiritual warfare in prayer, discovered God's will through prayer, made prayer the priority of His life, and prayed despite personal suffering. These four examples show Jesus praying about the same kinds of issues we often face as well. If Jesus insisted on a life of prayer to shape the contours of His life and ministry, how can His Church do less?

APOSTLES: ROLE MODELS IN PRAYER

I have always liked Acts 6:4, but I think I misunderstood it for years. The passage expresses a tremendous dependence on prayer that grew out of a real-life challenge.

The church was struggling with the administration of a large food distribution ministry to widows. Thousands of believers spread all over the city complicated the coordination of the daily food ministry. The meal ministry started out for all the right reasons but was poorly administered and was overlooking a large group of needy women.

Since the problem was widespread, it disrupted the fellowship of the early Church and threatened the larger ministry of evangelism. Eventually, the apostles were drawn into the expanding chasm being created, so they suggested a plan involving the appointment of additional Spirit-filled leaders to oversee the meal distribution ministry.

It was at that point the apostles turned the food ministry over to other qualified leaders and said, "But we will devote ourselves to prayer and to the ministry of the word" (Acts 6:4). The apostolic leaders clearly drew attention to the desired priority of their ministries, but their intended point may be far more expansive than we might think. When we read their words about devoting their lives to prayer, it's easy and almost natural to assume they meant private prayer. In fact, for years that's what I thought.

While we believe the apostles were men of prayer who learned the personal discipline directly from Jesus, there is more going on in Acts

6:4 than devotion to private prayer. The language of the New Testament brings clarity to this issue. In the Greek New Testament, the word *prayer* in verse four is preceded by a direct object "the" prayer. What the apostles were saying is not simply that they themselves prayed, but rather they would devote themselves to the prayer gatherings the Church had practiced since the upper room prayer meeting which preceded Pentecost (Acts 1:14).

This idea that the apostles saw the coordination and facilitation of the prayer meetings as part of the main business of their ministries fits much better with the idea they proposed. For instance, they also said they would devote themselves to the ministry of the Word. None of us believe they meant private study of the Word only. Instead, they clearly meant they would publicly preach and teach the Word. In the same way, they would not merely pray alone. Instead, they would work to coordinate congregational prayer meetings, which the Church had always viewed as the main power source of their progress. John Stott agrees with this when he wrote, "It is noteworthy that now the Twelve have added prayer to preaching (probably meaning public as well as private intercession) in specifying the essence of the apostles' ministry."[3]

A similar phrase in Acts 16:16 adds to our understanding of the way the word *prayer* is sometimes used in the Book of Acts. "As we were going to the place of prayer, we were met by a slave girl who had a spirit of divination and brought her owners much gain by fortune-telling" (Acts 16:16). The English Standard Version provides the sense of the passage, but the Greek text does not say the preachers were going to the "place of prayer." It says they were going to prayer. The word "place" is provided in English to round out the idea of the action being described. The fact is, the Greek word for *prayer* was used to describe not only the activity of prayer (as in 6:4) but also the place of prayer (as in 16:16) or even the organized prayer meetings.

For instance, in Acts 2:42, the Church ". . . devoted themselves to . . . the prayers." In that formational passage, "prayer" not only has the direct object ("the") but also the word for prayer is plural: "the prayers." In other words, "the prayers" refers to the organized prayer meetings so crucial to the discipleship of thousands of new believers. Clearly, the early Church devoted themselves to the prayer meetings! As Armin Gesswein said, "The early church didn't have a prayer meeting; the early church was the prayer meeting."[4]

There is one other observation we should examine. A further proof that the apostles were telling the Church their ministry would be devoted to organizing, maintaining, and facilitating congregational prayer is subtly demonstrated by a telling absence of the apostles in private prayer in the Book of Acts. If they had intended to suggest their ministries would be devoted to private prayer, we should expect to find multiple examples of the apostles in secret prayer—but we don't. With only one or two exceptions in Acts, every time we see the apostles in prayer, they are in prayer meetings.

From these passages, we discover an important element of ministry largely forgotten for too long but being recovered today: pastors should plan and lead dynamic prayer meetings that offer the only chance for real change some churches might ever experience. As we say repeatedly in our church, "Prayer meetings change the world." The apostles relied on prayer as the basis of their ministry. We should, too!

EARLY CHURCH: ROLE MODEL IN PRAYER

The Church was born in a prayer meeting. Admittedly, some of the prayer meetings we've attended over the years have borne little resemblance to the upper room of Acts, but we can recover the dynamism and passion of the infant Church. If we don't, we're doomed. Human strength has failed us. We must have a visitation of God again. The early Church model of frequent, desperate prayer meetings is our only way forward.

They were in a 10-day prayer meeting when the power of the Holy Spirit fell upon them and empowered them (Acts 1:14–2:21). Their experience of power was a direct answer to their prolonged prayer meeting. The 3,000 converts who were baptized that day were a direct result of Spirit-empowered preaching that grew out of desperate, congregational prayer. If we don't get what they got, it's only because we won't do what they did. Nothing will ever take the place of passionate prayer meetings.

Later, when the early Church faced potential setbacks, they did what came naturally; they retreated to a prayer meeting (Acts 4:23–31). They sought help from God because they believed God hears passionate prayer. The result of their prayer meeting was miraculous: "And when they had prayed, the place in which they were gathered together was shaken, and they were all filled with the Holy Spirit and continued to speak the word of God with boldness" (Acts 4:31). Once again, the power of God came to them as the result of a prayer meeting.

Before long, Peter, the recognized leader of the Church, was imprisoned. But Luke signals to his readers there was nothing to fear since the Church knew how to pray. "So Peter was kept in prison, but earnest prayer for him was made to God by the church" (Acts 12:5). Luke establishes a pattern throughout Acts that the early Church was a praying Church. The examples could go on, but perhaps from these few you see the pattern developing. Prayer meetings change the world!

HOW DOES IT WORK TODAY?

In Austin, Texas, pastors from all sized churches, different theological traditions, different racial backgrounds, and even different languages have united for nothing less than spiritual awakening in our time. This group of pastors has pressed forward with the belief that what God did before, He can do again. We lead thousands of believers across our city to trust God and make Austin the most prayed-for city in America!

How we're doing this is the urgent message of this book. It's more than a testimony about what God is doing in one unlikely place. The passion of our lives is to see a revival of desperate prayer sweep our nation until God pours out His blessings upon His people as never before, restores a deeply intrinsic burden for evangelism and New Testament Christian living, and sends a major spiritual awakening.

Will you join us?

Chapter Three

PASTORS OF PRAYER

By Trey Kent

I pastor Northwest Fellowship, a midsized church in Austin, Texas, that we started in 1993. There's nothing exceptional about our church or city—except for prayer. Now that we see how a city can be changed by ordinary, humble pastors and Christians who are willing to obey the call of Acts 1:14 to unify around prayer—and to do it unceasingly—our city is being overtaken by the power of prayer. Of course, there's more to seeing your city changed, but prayer is where it all begins.

John Burke, pastor and bestselling author of *Imagine Heaven* and *No Perfect People Allowed*, says: "I've been around Austin for 40 years, and I've never seen such unity among churches, favor in our city, or impact for the gospel—and I believe this movement of unceasing prayer undergirds it all."

The Austin story, comprised of normal people, normal pastors, normal churches—and an extraordinary God—is a 10-year history of God's grace through prayer. This is not a fad or a short-lived movement. Jesus is awakening His House of Prayer—the Church—in this hour. Here in Austin, we just experienced a decade of unceasing prayer that has forever changed my life, our family, our church, my ministry, and our city. We will never be the same.

The Unceasing Prayer Movement, a local church-based strategy, is spreading to cities and nations across the earth. Why? *Because it is Jesus' heart.* It is so simple and attainable. If your church sees Jesus as the answer to your city's problems, prayer can bring real and effective change.

These are the most exciting days to be alive! Our dream is to see Austin, Texas, become the most prayed-for city in America! It's also our dream that your city is transformed by unceasing prayer. It is so doable.

THE AUSTIN STORY

My part in this historic, decade-long prayer journey began with God speaking to me under a light pole in Austin, Texas, and culminated with confirmation during a night of worship and prayer in an upper room in Jerusalem, Israel. On February 18, 2008, my wife, Mary Anne, and I paused under that light pole while prayerwalking our neighborhood. In that moment, God spoke to me clearly about His desire for Austin to be covered in 24/7 prayer by area churches. I know it was God because I had never had such a thought. It landed with undeniable fire. It was a simple idea: 31 churches covering the city in 24/7 prayer with each church adopting one 24-hour day of prayer every month of the year.

That was it. It was a simple, reproducible, unifying, Jesus-exalting, God-sent idea to mobilize each church in Austin to be a praying church. After receiving this vision, I wondered about Scriptural support for the idea. Immediately I thought of 1 Thessalonians 5:17:

"Pray without ceasing." I learned very quickly that no one person can pray without ceasing on his or her own; we need each other to pray 24/7. Through this mutual support, I believe every church in American can be a praying church.

We are thrilled to see God moving in unprecedented ways in our city. Austin has been covered in 24/7, unceasing prayer by area churches for more than 10 years. We have about 100 churches in the greater Austin area who have adopted one day of prayer for our city every month. We host quarterly prayer meetings that have hundreds and sometimes thousands of believers across denominational lines meeting together to worship, pray, unify, and cry out for Jesus to change our city. We have Caucasian, Hispanic, African-American, and Asian churches united in a prayer movement that has brought true unity to a once openly divided city. We have yet to "arrive," but our city is more unified and transformed than I've seen it in the 25 years I've lived and pastored in Austin.

The vision for unceasing prayer in your city begins with a pastor or pastors. This was a shocking thought for our city. Very few pastors were leading their churches to be praying churches for the city. Most pastors didn't see themselves as the key to a movement of prayer. Often, pastors delegate prayer to intercessors, prayer teams, and other prayer-driven ministries. Yet, this movement of prayer begins and ends with local church pastors who are the key to raising up and maintaining praying churches that will literally transform our cities.

Most pastors begin by mobilizing 24 people to adopt one hour of prayer, thus covering a full day of prayer. It's the beauty of this simple prayer model! Every church, large or small, can adopt a half or a full day of prayer. This allows pastors to highlight the vital importance of prayer at least once a month and to continue the process of building a culture of prayer in their churches.

OVERCOMING SKEPTICISM

At our first Unceasing Prayer Pastors Luncheon in 2008, we cast the vision for pastors and churches to adopt a day of prayer for our city in the coming year. Rick Randall, the pastor at Austin Cornerstone Church, stood up and said, "I don't think every church is to be a praying church like this, and I don't believe we are all gifted to be intercessors."

It was not one of our best moments in spreading the vision. We recovered from the comment and got at least a dozen churches to adopt a day. As Randall was leaving the meeting, his dear friend Pastor Geno Hildebrandt of Hope Chapel said he "guilted" Randall into involvement by suggesting, "Why don't you adopt 12 hours, a half-day of prayer, and we will adopt the other 12 hours. We will split our day of prayer." Randall begrudgingly agreed—and then the miracle began. As he led his church to pray for our city that half day a month, God began to ignite his heart and the church's heart!

Pastor Randall's story doesn't end there. He began leading his church in adopting a full day of prayer every month, but he also called his church to an even more radical pursuit of God. One day he called me and invited me to attend 24 hours of prayer at his church. I wasn't sure what he meant because it didn't seem any different from our normal strategy. He patiently explained that his church had a slightly different plan. They invited their entire congregation to come to the building to pray together for 24 straight hours. No one was going to leave!

I went to that historic prayer gathering. Fifty-five of us stayed and prayed non-stop together for 24 hours. It not only changed me but revealed clearly what God can do with a resistant pastor who simply adopts a day of prayer for the city. Randall led his church through nine months of intense prayer. They had prayer meetings morning, noon, and night, praying for the lost to be saved and for believers to be salt and light. At the end of the nine-month season, around 300 people had come to Christ. The power of prayer was on display!

Pastor Randall joined our newly formed Unceasing Prayer Leadership Team in 2011. He is now spreading a passion for prayer into once untouched areas of the city of Austin. He is the senior chaplain for the Austin Police Department and is helping to bring unprecedented change as he serves our city and city leaders.

This is critically important, because right now, in your city, there are pastors who are prepared to lead their churches in 24/7 prayer for spiritual awakening. The goal is full-on revival for the city, driven by men and women who have laid down their agendas to unify for a greater move of God citywide. We don't believe the adage that "prayer is for some churches but not for others." We believe that when Jesus called His Church a house of prayer for all nations, He meant *every* church.

THE REST OF THE TEAM

Let me introduce you to the other five team members who joined Randall and me to lead the Unceasing Prayer Movement in Austin.

David Smith, the executive director of the Austin Baptist Association, joined us in 2011, and the three of us formed the nucleus of the original Unceasing Prayer Leadership Team. Dr. Smith serves 200 Southern Baptist churches in the area, and is a key unifier, team player, and powerful agent to spread the vision for unceasing prayer, both locally and beyond. He says this about his involvement:

> The Unceasing Prayer Ministry in Austin that God birthed over 10 years ago has been one of the highlights of my ministry here as the executive director of the Austin Baptist Association. As associational director, I am tasked with casting a vision for our association of churches that can only come

> about as we work together. In the case of unceasing prayer, it can't be accomplished as one church or even as one denomination. It requires the Body of Christ to come together. Unceasing prayer is essential to the vitality of our relationship to the Lord and our ability to function in this world. Unceasing prayer is that continually ascending prayer that sees every aspect of life as an opportunity to commune with God.

Will Davis, senior pastor of Austin Christian Fellowship, leads six church campuses and has written extensively on prayer. Davis joined our team in 2014, bringing a wealth of knowledge and experience in prayer. He is a lifelong Austinite whose father has a significant legacy in the city through law and politics. Pastor Davis brings a relational equity in our city second to none. At a recent prayer gathering for leaders, Davis said, "PBS just did a documentary on Austin featuring *South by Southwest* and how Austin became *weird*. They missed that the real story of our city is how Austin became the most prayed-for city in America and how a new generation of leaders are rising up to change our city."

Kie Bowman, a national Southern Baptist leader and pastor of Hyde Park Baptist Church in Austin, joined the Unceasing Prayer team in 2014 when our city water source was at a historic low. You will read the full story later, but this crisis caused pastors to come together to host a citywide prayer meeting at Hyde Park Baptist. One thousand area believers gathered and cried out all evening for rain and revival. Dr. Bowman not only hosted the prayer meeting, but became a key player in spreading a passion for God through personal prayer, prayer meetings, and writing numerous books equipping believers to become more fruitful disciples. Bowman's passion for prayer and the prayer movement is unprecedented. He's also the co-author of this book.

Abraham Perez joined the Unceasing Prayer team in 2014. He

is a national Hispanic leader who pastors Reconciliation Church in Austin, and equips pastors through his Healthy Pastors Grow ministry. Pastor Perez has done more to mobilize area Hispanic pastors toward unity and prayer than any other leader in our city. His church is serious about prayer; they have maintained two hours of corporate prayer, seven days a week for 12 years, and counting.

According to Perez, "Unceasing prayer has been the vehicle to unify pastors and churches in our city to intercede for revival. The movement has brought unity to many pastors who were isolated and doing church all by themselves. We have become a body and a team to intercede for our city."

Jordan Mkwanazi, originally from Zimbabwe, is the senior pastor of Metropolitan African Methodist Episcopal Church (AME) in downtown Austin. He's a seasoned pastor with a deep heart for God and His people. We met Mkwanazi shortly after the tragic Charleston, South Carolina, church shooting in 2015. After the death of nine African American believers who were attending a Bible study at Emmanuel AME Church, we were compelled to hold a prayer meeting in Austin at the exact time of the shooting one week after the murders occurred. Pastor Mkwanazi graciously hosted our prayer meeting. With only a few days' notice, hundreds of area believers stood in solidarity to pray, unify, and worship Jesus together. This overflow crowd was a sign and a wonder to our city.

Shortly after this event, Mkwanazi joined our team. He is doing a phenomenal job leading his church to build a culture of prayer. He explains their journey: "Metropolitan AME Church has shifted towards becoming a church that embraces a culture of prayer. We have moved from Wednesday night prayer meetings to overnight prayer gatherings, to having every Monday morning intercessory prayer. Prayer has become the center stage of our ministry. We are evolving as a church into fearless, bold, and committed prayer warriors."

AN UNREALIZED OPPORTUNITY

The list of Austin area pastors who have helped us pray more than 87,600 nonstop hours (24/7 for 10 years) for our city is literally in the hundreds! They include Bible churches, Methodist, non-denominational, Assembly of God, Southern Baptist, and on and on—all committed to Jesus transforming our city through praying for unity according to John 17 and revival in keeping with 2 Chronicles 7:14: "if my people who are called by my name humble themselves, and pray and seek my face and turn from their wicked ways, then I will hear from heaven and will forgive their sin and heal their land."

In September 2017, Pastor Jim Cymbala of Brooklyn Tabernacle returned to Austin for a second time to lead pastors in a day of training and prayer. The day before the event, our Unceasing Prayer team, under Kie Bowman's leadership, invited national and citywide prayer leaders to attend a one-day round table discussing the prayer movement across America. We were blessed to have Ronnie Floyd, senior pastor of Cross Church and president of the National Day of Prayer; Dave Butts, chairman of the National Prayer Committee; and other key prayer leaders across America join us. It was an extraordinary time.

As I reflect on the event, one key message consistently rang true as leaders spoke: *This is the season for senior pastors nationwide to rise up and lead their churches to become praying churches.* This, we all agree, is not only the missing link but is the astounding opportunity awaiting us in our great land!

Praying pastors who establish their churches as houses of prayer are leading the greatest army ever mobilized in world-history—the local church.

Chapter Four

A CULTURE OF PRAYER

By Trey Kent

I remember listening to a recording of Jim Cymbala's classic sermon, "My House Shall Be Called a House of Prayer," that he preached in Indianapolis in 1994. I was awestruck by the power and simplicity of the truths he proclaimed. Cymbala rightly says that while people gripe about prayer being taken out of schools, the true tragedy is that prayer has been taken out of our churches! This painful truth is devastating, but there is hope. If Jesus calls us to be a house of prayer for all nations, then He has placed inside the heart of those born of His Spirit the desire to be a people of prayer. And the quickest way to build a people of prayer is to intentionally develop a culture of prayer. That's the focus of this chapter.

From the early pages of Genesis to the later letters of Paul, the people of God are known as those who call upon the Lord:

- "Seth also had a son, and he named him Enosh. At that time people began to call on the name of the Lord" (Gen. 4:26).

- So flee youthful passions and pursue righteousness, faith, love, and peace, along with those who call on the Lord from a pure heart" (2 Tim. 2:22).

We are first and foremost those who call upon the Lord. Jesus Christ died, rose again, and poured out His Spirit upon the Church so we can be in relationship with Him. At the heart of true relationship is prayer. It's important that we not ignore this most critical aspect of what it means to be a child of God. We can't relegate prayer as a side issue when prayer is *the* issue. It's the place where believers are filled afresh and anew with the very life of God.

When the early disciples faced intense persecution after being released from jail, Peter and John gathered with other believers and did what all true believers do—they cried out to God together! When they were released, they went to their friends and reported what the chief priests and the elders had said to them:

> And when they heard it, they lifted their voices together to God and said, "Sovereign Lord, who made the heaven and the earth and the sea and everything in them, who through the mouth of our father David, your servant, said by the Holy Spirit, 'Why did the Gentiles rage, and the peoples plot in vain? The kings of the earth set themselves, and the rulers were gathered together, against the Lord and against his Anointed'— for truly in this city there were gathered together against your holy servant Jesus, whom you anointed, both Herod and Pontius Pilate, along with the Gentiles and the peoples of Israel, to do whatever your hand and your plan had predestined to take place. And now, Lord, look upon their threats and grant to your servants to continue to speak your word with all boldness, while you

> stretch out your hand to heal, and signs and wonders are performed through the name of your holy servant Jesus." And when they had prayed, the place in which they were gathered together was shaken, and they were all filled with the Holy Spirit and continued to speak the word of God with boldness. (Acts 4:24–31)

KEY LESSONS IN BUILDING CULTURE

How do we build this culture of prayer in our local churches? I'll lean on the wisdom of three seasoned pastors who not only turned their respective churches into houses of prayer, but have helped other pastors establish prayer more deeply into the fabric of church life: Ronnie Floyd, president of Southern Baptist Executive Committee (SBC), Jim Cymbala of Brooklyn Tabernacle, and Daniel Henderson of Strategic Renewal.

Floyd's passion for prayer was evident as he pastored Cross Church for 32 years, long before his recent role as president of the National Day of Prayer Task Force or his new role with the SBC. He stands as a beacon of light concerning the vital importance of prayer and praying churches. Kie Bowman and I recently joined Floyd to speak at Cross Church in Springdale, Arkansas, for the National Day of Prayer Leadership Summit. I asked Floyd his thoughts on building a culture of prayer in the local church. Here's his response:

> The pastor is the key to creating a culture of prayer in the local church. I believe there are two ways a pastor can really lead his people to believe in prayer: (1) Begin to pray aloud for the people with great passion in the public Sunday morning worship services; yes, we need to return to the value of the pastoral prayer in worship services weekly. (2) Once every 12 to 18 months, turn the entire Sunday

> morning worship services into a planned prayer meeting that will engage the masses in prayer. Again, as the pastor goes, so goes the church. Stop delegating prayer to others. Lead your church to be a praying church.

Dr. Floyd is urging pastors to make prayer prominent again in the Sunday morning worship experience of their local church. Pastor Cymbala agrees. At the close of his book, *Fresh Wind, Fresh Fire*, (one of the most inspiring books you'll read and a must-read for every church desiring to build a culture of prayer), he advises:

> Many times the spirit of prayer has been so absent in a church that a weeknight prayer meeting, no matter how biblical or laudable, meets with apathy and coldness. . . . I often recommend that those pastors adjust the Sunday service instead. Preaching time can be shortened somewhat; and when the sermon is over, invite those who feel touched by the Word to come forward for prayer. Get your staff and the church's spiritual leaders around you and pray with them. What is an altar service? It's a mini-prayer meeting.

This will work. Simply shorten the service and leave time for various kinds of prayer at the end. We do this at Northwest Fellowship and have experienced the power of these moments.

Praying pastors lead to praying churches, and praying churches lead to transformed cities! Daniel Henderson, founder of Strategic Renewal and 6:4 Fellowship, has been mentoring pastors and churches for decades. He led our Austin area Pastor Prayer Gathering in 2011. Pastors were profoundly impacted as Henderson led a preconference session on building a culture of prayer in your local church. He shared the following seven points—and each has changed our church and equipped churches throughout America:

1. A prayer culture is not a prayer program.
2. A prayer culture always emanates from the epicenter of church leadership.
3. A prayer culture is fueled by experience, not explanation.
4. A prayer culture is rooted in clarity and conviction about community.
5. A prayer culture is sustained by the right motives.
6. A prayer culture is a key to supernatural mission accomplishment.
7. A prayer culture is more of a crockpot than a microwave.

The most vital principle for our church has been point number two: "A culture of prayer always emanates from the epicenter of church leadership." In Henderson's words, "You will never build a culture of prayer unless church leadership buys in."

If the church leadership has a culture of prayer built into their lives, marriages, families, and ministries, the culture will be further embraced by the congregation at large. From personal experience, I can assure you it's a battle! Our staff meetings, elder meetings, and leader meetings must be saturated with times of serious and extended prayer. As Henderson's point three maintains: "a prayer culture is fueled by experience." Many of us as preachers try to "teach" prayer into people without letting them "experience" it.

CATCHING PRAYER

I recall a disappointing story of a pastor who preached 52 weeks in a row on prayer and, sadly, had even less of a prayer culture than when he started! Why? Because those who heard all those sermons thought, *I'll never be good enough to pray like that.*

We've discovered the key is to invite people to pray together weekly in small prayer meetings. This gives them the opportunity to both *catch* prayer and to begin crying out to God in their own words and way. There's nothing like it.

For example, at a recent Unceasing Prayer Day at our church, Kathy, one of our seasoned prayer warriors, said she'd like to schedule her prayer hour with someone who had never prayed for an hour. A common question asked when we launched unceasing prayer was, "How can I possibly pray for a full hour?" The answer is always to let people try it—and keep a good prayer guide close by. Kathy's desire to include a "newbie" came from an experience she'd enjoyed several years before as she shared her hour of prayer with a woman named Chris, who'd never prayed in this manner and thought herself completely unable to fulfill the mission. Kathy testified that Chris prayed almost the entire time with no guidance. She just needed someone there to encourage her. Chris is now one of our faithful prayer warriors on our day of prayer. She's also become an effective prayer warrior for her family as they face times of great difficulty. She is a matriarch of prayer!

Adopting a day of prayer every month to pray for your city is the most effective way to begin and maintain a culture of prayer in your local church. After this is established and growing, other steps can be taken. We encourage Austin area churches to start with at least 24 people each adopting one hour of prayer to cover a day. In time, increase the numbers to two or three people per hour.

After four years of this model, we believed the next step was to invite our prayer warriors to come to our church prayer room to pray together on our day of prayer. This has been a very effective strategy, as it has given a great opportunity for our church to unite in prayer for our city. My beautiful wife, Mary Anne, and I adopted midnight as our hour so that we can kick off our church's day of prayer together. Soon Danny, the husband of our prayer warrior Kathy, joined us at midnight. He's been our faithful prayer partner for eight years. Just recently, Rita joined us at midnight. Now four of us cry out together for Jesus to change our city!

THE NEXT STEP OF FAITH

What's next? After your church adopts a day of prayer each month and grows it to several people per hour, you need to answer this question: *What's the next step of faith in prayer God is calling us to take?*

It is different for every church. Some focus on prayerwalking their neighborhoods and city. Others establish one or more prayer meetings in their local church. The bravest do overnight prayer meetings. The sky is the limit! Ask God to help you build a culture of prayer in your local church that can involve everyone.

At Northwest Fellowship, we began by doing all-night prayer meetings. Sometimes our church prayed alone and other times we partnered with sister churches. We then established weekly prayer meetings. We didn't fully understand what we were doing, but we chose to establish several smaller prayer meetings rather than having one large prayer meeting. This decision was made because of the scattered nature of our members' schedules in the greater Austin area. Later, we discovered what may be the most important reason to have smaller prayer meetings: people participate at a higher level when prayer meetings have 10 or fewer people. The goal is to have everyone contribute to the prayer times.

Dr. Jason Hubbard, the founder and director of Lighthouse World Prayer Center in Bellingham, Washington, helped me understand this strategy. They have 30 weekly prayer meetings with various emphases that are attended by 10 or so believers. Each gets to participate and be an active part of building the greater Bellingham canopy of prayer. Interesting fact: Hubbard launched 24/7 prayer in Bellingham using the same strategy we employed in Austin on the exact same day, January 1, 2009. Both cities have experienced more than a decade of unceasing prayer! Hubbard and I had never met until we were both almost nine years into our respective, identical 24/7 prayer strategies. We both know it was God's idea, not ours. Jesus wants His cities covered in 24/7 prayer until He returns!

Praying pastors leading a growing prayer culture are vitally important. But what does it mean to be a people of prayer, both individually and corporately? Hopefully that will become clear in the rest of the book.

Chapter Five

PRAYER MOVEMENTS IGNITING REVIVAL FIRES

By Kie Bowman

Life is simultaneously uncertain and predictable. It is uncertain because circumstances can change as suddenly as the Texas weather. On the other hand, we often notice patterns in life; we recognize a certain natural predictability.

For instance, one morning my wife asked me a funny question, especially considering our marriage of several years: "Why do you beat your cereal?"

I laughed, because all my life I have tapped my breakfast cereal with my spoon. (I don't like the cereal floating on top of the milk; I want it all equally submerged, so I tap it.) After listening to the same monotonous rhythm for years, my wife finally couldn't stand it one more morning. Oddly, I do it subconsciously, habitually, and predictably. So, if my wife sees me pour a bowl of cereal, she knows what's coming: tap, tap, tap, tap, tap.

We can often predict outcomes based on patterns. What happened before might be an indicator of what happens next. For instance, computer algorithms routinely demonstrate the reliability of patterns in almost every area of life.

When I connect my smartphone in the car, computer algorithms predict where I might be headed based on my previous, frequent trips. The "Frequent Locations" feature in my phone automatically suggests where it *thinks* I'm going. Sometimes the algorithm suggests how far it is to the grocery store where my wife and I shop. On other days, the smartphone automatically predicts the traffic flow and the distance to my office. It's an amazing part of life today. I didn't program or ask my phone. The built-in computer runs algorithms and predicts my moves based on repeated habits.

What if there is an algorithm to revival? Admittedly, many will object to this question because revival is a work of our sovereign God. He can never be manipulated, and I agree with that. On the other hand, our sovereign God has established principles of order and patterns in all of creation. Those principles of predictability never negate His sovereignty.

One indicator of revival is prayer. Where revivals and awakenings have occurred in the past, we notice they were preceded by prayer movements or extraordinary prayers by individuals or groups. It's been said that history is silent about revivals that did not begin in prayer.

That's why I believe we are in the early stages of a massive move of God. Why? History demonstrates that periods of revival are always preceded by prayer movements. Since we are in a global prayer movement of epic proportions, what might God be preparing for the world? If what He did in the past is a clue, we may be headed for the greatest spiritual awakening in history.

PRAYER MOVEMENTS IN SCRIPTURE

Prayer (talking with God) is as old as Adam and Eve. It first took place in Eden when God walked with man through the garden "in the cool of the day" (Gen. 3:8). Then a couple of generations later, some version of a consistent, organized prayer meeting emerged: "At that time people began to call upon the name of the Lord" (Gen. 4:26). That was the beginning of the prayer movement! In fact, the first time in Scripture we find an entire group of people dedicated to the worship of God, the characteristic that defined them was prayer: they "called on the name of the Lord."

A lot has changed since that "pre-flood" prayer movement, but God remains the same and still invites His people "to call upon the name of the Lord." In fact, there have been numerous prayer movements in the history of the Church, and we are in one now. Some people, even many Christians, are somehow unaware of the current global prayer movement. However, once one becomes aware of it, the prayer movement is impossible to ignore.

Maybe we have largely ignored prayer movements because we're natural activists rather than contemplatives. In any case, significant prayer movements in history are often overshadowed by exciting, louder events which are apparently more dramatic, even though prayer usually makes those exciting and dramatic events possible.

We must never forget, in our rush to action, that Jesus considered prayer an action. In fact, it was so important He instructed the apostles to "stay in the city until you are clothed with power from on high" (Luke 24:49).

The apostles and the rest of Jesus' followers obviously interpreted "stay" as a call to unceasing prayer. Luke tells us they split their time between being "continually in the temple blessing God" and praying in a large upper room "devoting themselves to prayer" (Luke 24:53;

Acts 1:12–14). After 10 days of unceasing prayer, the Holy Spirit filled them all—and nothing has been the same since!

The Church of Jesus began in an unceasing prayer movement in an upper room in Jerusalem, Israel, in the warm days of late spring, just 50 days after the resurrection of Jesus. Jim Cymbala reminds us of the importance of prayer in the Church when he states, "Jesus launched the Christian Church, not while someone was preaching, but while the people were praying."[5]

Throughout the history of the Church, when we've needed correction or renewal, God has called us back to "an upper room." He is obviously doing that again now. But before we examine the current prayer movement, let's establish a frame of reference by glancing at some of the more prominent and dynamic movements of the past.

ONE HUNDRED YEARS OF UNCEASING PRAYER

While the outpouring of God's Spirit accompanied by fire, the sound of hurricane-force winds, and every person in the room fluently preaching in foreign languages they had never learned hasn't ever occurred again, there is a model for us woven into the biblical narrative of Pentecost. Powerful, persistent prayer meetings, like the one that preceded Pentecost, always prepare the Church for greater effectiveness.

For instance, on August 27, 1727, a group of spiritual refugees made a commitment to unceasing prayer with far reaching effects. The group launched a 24-hour prayer ministry that lasted non-stop for 100 years.[6]

The link between the Moravian's 100-year prayer meeting and one of the greatest eras of Christian expansion and advancement in history cannot be shrugged aside as mere coincidence. After all, as a former archbishop of Canterbury is reported to have said, "When I pray, coincidences happen, and when I don't, they don't."[7]

In the early 1700s, because of religious persecution against Protestants in Europe, Count Nicolaus Ludwig von Zinzendorf, a wealthy, young German nobleman with strong pietistic leanings, started receiving spiritual outcasts at his estate. Before long, 300 people from Moravia (the modern Czech Republic) had migrated to the count's estate in Saxony, which later came to be known as Herrnhut (meaning the Lord's Watch). The pietistic emphasis on prayer eventually led 24 men and 24 women from the group to commit to one hour of prayer each for 24 hours. Their passion for prayer inspired generations of "spiritual descendants," with the prayer vigil lasting continuously for 100 years.[8]

The results of the Moravian prayer meeting can be measured in at least three ways. For one, a prayer meeting that lasts 100 years is a success by any standard! Next, the Moravians (the praying community at Herrnhut) sent out foreign missionaries almost 70 years before William Carey launched the modern mission movement. In fact, the Baptist mission movement was partially inspired by the international passion of the Moravians. When the Baptist movement launched in 1793, they were overheard to say, "Look what those Moravians had done."[9]

Finally, it's eye-opening to consider the advancement of Christianity during that 100-year period. That era saw some of the most significant developments in Christian history.

For instance, the American Colonies experienced the First Great Awakening beginning in the early 1700s. It was an act of God spurred by a prayer movement and the ministries of godly leaders like Jonathan Edwards and others, who were committed to prayer.[10]

The First Great Awakening, as a movement, was deeply influenced by George Whitefield, whose evangelistic ministry helped tie local revivals into a national awakening. Whitefield was originally assisted in his work in America by Moravians, who had come from Herrnhut to do mission work among Native Americans.[11]

On the other side of the Atlantic, John Wesley was converted at a Moravian Bible study and prayer meeting at Aldersgate, London, England, in 1738. He went on to lead the evangelical awakening in Britain and founded the Methodist movement.[12]

The slave trade was abolished in England in 1807, and the Moravian prayer movement was indirectly related. The young British politician William Wilberforce was converted under the ministry of John Wesley (who was led to Christ by the Moravians). Wesley was opposed to slavery, and on his deathbed wrote what was to be his last letter. That historic letter was to William Wilberforce, urging him to use his position to end slavery.[13]

During the 100-year Moravian prayer meeting, the Second Great Awakening in America also occurred. It was undergirded by prayer after several leaders reread Jonathan Edwards' book on a call for revival, in which he calls for extraordinary prayer.[14] Prayer obviously played a significant role in the early American awakenings.

All the Christian advances mentioned here barely scratch the surface of the century of revival and missions between the early 1700s to the early 1800s. But one thing is clear—behind every advance was an extraordinary international prayer movement fervently praying for gospel advancement around the world.

Few movements have been as influential or effective as the Moravian 100-year prayer meeting. The century during which the Moravians prayed for God's Kingdom to expand saw one of the most effective periods for the Church of Jesus in modern history. I believe it is impossible to disregard the role prayer played in these significant moments in the life of the Church. It is time to light the fires of prayer movements again.

PRAYER IN NEW YORK

Imagine this scenario: Church attendance and influence has been in decline for more than a decade. Part of the problem is brought about by the public failures of a few Christians who have brought ridicule, and increased cynicism, about the Church on a national scale. In addition, America is in an unprecedented period of economic prosperity. Under the surface, however, issues of race and equality are tearing at the fabric of the country. Sound familiar?

This describes the decade in America before national, spiritual awakening burst on the scene across the nation in 1857–1858.[15] What turned America toward God? Surprisingly, a prayer meeting lit the fuse of explosive spiritual change across the entire United States.

Like many other churches, the Old North Dutch Reformed Church on Fulton Street in Lower Manhattan near the financial district was in trouble. Attendance sunk lower every year. The financial success of the country was partly a factor. As people made more money, they could afford to flee the downtown districts and find better living conditions elsewhere in the city.[16] As a result, members who moved to more family-friendly suburbs didn't return to downtown churches on Sunday. Church leaders knew something had to be done, so in July 1857 the church leaders hired a tall, quiet businessman to become a city missionary to Lower Manhattan.[17]

Jeremiah Lanphier started printing flyers and inviting people to church, but was soon out of money and ideas. Nothing worked. Lanphier had left the mercantile industry in Lower Manhattan to help his church, so he instinctively understood the lifestyle of the downtown business community. One day while walking the streets, he noticed how anxious, restless, and tired the average New Yorker looked. As he studied their faces, the thought came to Lanphier that a noontime prayer meeting might offer a refreshing encouragement to the businessmen.[18]

The noon prayer meetings triggered a national spiritual awakening within months. At this point, we might assume Lanphier was a creative genius with the insight of a futurist, but the idea of prayer meetings in business districts was already occurring in large cities. In fact, churches in Boston had been hosting similar daily prayer meetings, along with quarterly calls for days of fasting, for more than six years before Lanphier launched his prayer meeting in Manhattan.[19] The objective of those persistent, daily prayer meetings was an outpouring of the Holy Spirit, leading to revival.[20]

Then, in early spring of 1857, a wealthy Christian businessman from New York attended a prayer meeting in Boston and determined to start something similar in New York City. As a result, following his lead, a group of pastors in Brooklyn urged church leaders across New York City to start prayer meetings. Lanphier started one at the Old North Dutch Reformed Church near the financial district.

One of America's most transformative, spiritual events soon began following the same structure and guidelines as were common in the Boston meetings, with the exception of the time. Previous prayer meetings had been in the morning, while Lanphier invited people during the noon hour.[21]

It is reasonable to conclude from the evidence that America's greatest prayer movement was preceded by a prayer movement! Samuel Chadwick was right, "The greatest answer to prayer is more prayer."

At noon on September 23, 1857, Lanphier opened the third floor of the church on Fulton Street for the first prayer meeting. For 30 minutes, he sat praying alone. Finally, at 12:30 p.m. he was joined by a few others—six total on the first day. Of the six, four different denominations were represented. When real revival comes, denominational distinctions among Christian brothers take a back seat to the higher purpose of calling upon the Lord in desperate prayer. A week later, 20 men attended. The third week, nearly 40 met. By October 14, about 100 men were in attendance, and many were unconverted.[22] The presence of lost people fueled the incredible evangelistic results produced through the prayer meetings.

Within six months, as many as 50,000 people were attending daily prayer meetings across New York City. By the end of 1858, prayer meetings spread across the United States.[23] Revival had come. That's our hope today. Prayer meetings change the world.

According to J. Edwin Orr, "Within two years, a million converts were added to the American churches. No part of the nation remained untouched by fervent prayer."[24]

All we can say in Austin is, "Lord, do it again!" We are leading prayer meetings and covering our city in 24/7 prayer because we believe mere human attempts bring only human results. We are desperate to see God move to transform our city. So we pray.

PRAYER THAT PRECEDED THE GREATEST AWAKENING

The Welsh Revival of 1904–1905 was the most far-reaching of any modern awakening. Five months after the revival began, there were 100,000 conversions in Wales![25] The scope of the Welsh Revival reached much farther than the incredible early results. Not only did revival radically affect Wales, it slipped beyond the confines of its origin in the coal mining community and touched the world.

In many ways, the Welsh Revival was built for *portability* and ease of travel. Its entire expression lacked typical structures that might have anchored it to one locale. Instead, it was a phenomenon of the Spirit's outpouring; everything was somewhat unpredictable.

The famous British pastor, G. Campbell Morgan from London, visited the revival services with Evan Roberts (a leader in the revival movement) many times. Morgan's large evangelical church was just a block from Buckingham Palace and the embodiment of British evangelical reservation and deportment. When Morgan reported on the revival, he was simultaneously confused and blessed by the lack of visible structure. He called the entire experience "Pentecost continued" and added, ". . . there is no preaching, no order, no hymnbooks, no choirs, no organs, no collections, and finally no advertising. . . . There were organs, but silent; the ministers, but among the rest of the people, rejoicing and prophesying with the rest, only there was no preaching. . . . No choir did I say? It was all choir. And hymns! I stood and listened in wonder and amazement at that congregation on that night singing hymn after hymn, long hymns, sung without hymnbooks. . . . No advertising. The whole thing advertises itself. . . ."[26]

No wonder the movement easily adapted itself to manifestations in other countries. Numerous preachers, such as the previously mentioned Morgan, came to witness it, perhaps out of curiosity. They wanted to see firsthand the stories emanating out of Wales. Those same preachers returned home with a zeal to see the fire of revival in their own countries—and the revival spread.

When we read Morgan's description, it actually sounds more like a modern, worship-driven prayer meeting than an organized evangelistic service. In fact, the movement was born and sustained in prayer.

Evan Roberts was the leading minister associated with the Welsh Revival. He was primarily a man obsessed with prayer and the presence of God. He was only 27 years old when the revival started.

Roberts spent most of his young life in prayer. For more than a decade prior to the revival, he attended prayer meetings several nights a week. Other young men enjoyed going to the beach for boating and recreation. Seeing them naturally tempted Roberts to join them. Yet he resisted because he was committed to prayer for revival. Every night, Monday through Friday, Roberts attended prayer meetings in different locations. Then at home during one three-month period, he would kneel beside his bed for four hours of private prayer each night from about 1:00–5:00 a.m.[27]

It was at prayer meetings where Roberts experienced unusually powerful visitations of the Holy Spirit. These experiences, fueled by years of prayer, catapulted him into the public eye as the leader of the revival.

By 1906, having given his entire life to prayer meetings and speaking, and after having been thrust into the uncomfortable circumstance of international recognition and the accompanying criticism that comes with it, the young Roberts was fatigued to the point of exhaustion. He retreated from the public eye and spent most of the rest of his life in seclusion.

Concerns about his mental health, due in part to fatigue and depression, were warranted. He was clearly fragile during those years. Yet he said of his self-imposed exile, "My work is devoted to prayer. By preaching I would reach the limited few, but by and through prayer I can reach the whole of mankind for God. But I am afraid people do not understand what all this means and what it involves."[28]

It's difficult to calculate how much Evan Roberts' life of intercession and secret prayer affected the revival that had begun with young, praying leaders in Wales and spread around the world. But it is clear from the record, the greatest of all the awakenings began and was sustained by a spirit of intercession and prayer.

The next phase of revival history involves the modern prayer movement and leads us up to the current moment. Our hearts are thrilled by stories of past revivals preceded by prayer movements. But no period in history is more exciting than what God is doing now.

Chapter Six

PRAYER NOW

By Kie Bowman

The Jesus Movement was the biggest news in American Christianity in 1971. One example of the media fascination with the youth revival was the psychedelic painting of Jesus that summer on the cover of *Time* magazine. The caption said it all: "The Jesus Revolution."[29]

In the late 1960s and early 1970s, an unusual movement of hippies, with newfound, conservative Christian beliefs, started spreading from the hippie haven of Haight-Ashbury in San Francisco to the warm beaches of Southern California.[30] Inexplicably, in February 1970, in the chapel services of Asbury College in Wilmore, Kentucky (a place that probably represented the sociological opposite pole from San Francisco), a spontaneous, non-stop prayer meeting and revival rocked the campus and spread to other campuses across the country.[31]

What fueled these apparently sudden revival movements? The answer is a complex mix of spiritual and social dynamics, but missiologist C. Peter Wagner supplies one significant component: About the time the first hippies were coming to Christ, a prayer movement was beginning.[32]

Prayer movements are quieter than tens of thousands of young people coming to Christ in a short window of time. They grow from unnoticed tributaries of prayer to rushing rivers of revival over time. In fact, the current prayer movement in the United States is most likely a direct result of what began around 1970. It seems best to examine the prayer movement in two phases.

THE ORGANIZATIONAL PHASE (1970-1999)

It's clear from even a cursory review of our recent history that something changed in the early 1970s. A flurry of activity and interdenominational cooperation helped launch the early phase of the current prayer movement. In those earliest days, the focus was understandably on more traditional approaches involving boards, committees, and corporate structures. For instance, in 1974 the National Prayer Committee was launched as the prayer sub-committee of the Lausanne International Congress on World Evangelization. Vonette Bright, the co-founder, along with her husband, Bill, of Campus Crusade for Christ (now Cru), was chosen as the first leader.[33] America's National Prayer Committee (NPC) was officially organized in 1979.

The NPC proved to be a major puzzle piece in the multi-faceted prayer movement God was fitting together. Other members of the NPC included Dick Eastman, who played a major role in the early phase of the prayer movement. He became the president of the NPC, wrote prayer books, and launched a school of prayer that has reached into 120 nations.[34]

By 1981, the NPC, after consistent effort, had conceived of a robust plan involving the National Day of Prayer. They worked relentlessly until finally, in 1988, President Ronald Reagan signed into law what is known as The National Day of Prayer.[35]

By the early 1990s, there was a growing sense that America needed revival and spiritual awakening. Organizations like the National Day of Prayer were busy mobilizing awareness for prayer. Books were written on prayer, including Eastman's *The Hour that Changes the World* and *Look What God Is Doing!* that have sold more than two million copies. In addition, Eastman launched the Change the World School of Prayer in Colorado Springs where he trained more than two million people to pray.[36]

Churches around the country were focusing time and energy on prayer, too. Jim Cymbala was transforming Brooklyn Tabernacle to be a *house of prayer* in a groundbreaking way. Following the direction of the Spirit in the 1970s, he led a handful of believers to make prayer the core of the struggling, inner-city congregation in Brooklyn. Eventually thousands of people attended the church and its Tuesday night prayer gathering.[37] Rarely had a modern church been so totally committed to prayer as a strategy for living the Christian life and doing ministry. The results were not only changing Brooklyn but also influencing pastors and churches in other places as they heard about the miracle of Brooklyn Tabernacle's revival and growth because of prayer.

Another remarkable prayer movement in Queens in New York City developed during the late 1980s. Desperation over the spiritual and social conditions of the city led 75 churches to join in *concerts of prayer.*[38] Pockets of praying people swimming against the tide of the status quo could be found bubbling up in apparently random places.

Still, even with all the growing passion for prayer, there seemed to be a need for a catalytic event to ignite the fire of prayer into a national movement. The catalyst occurred in 1994. when Bill Bright invited Christian leaders to join him in Orlando, Florida, for three days of prayer and fasting.[39]

In response to his call, 600 Christian leaders from numerous branches of the Christian family tree arrived. The agenda was simple: *Pray and fast for spiritual awakening in America.* It was the largest convocation of its kind in United States history. Never had so many leaders representing so many denominations gathered to repent, fast, and pray.[40]

God seemed to be speaking to His Body in an urgent and clear fashion. Those in attendance were aware something unique was happening—and that more would happen as a result. Chuck Colson called the prayer meeting "the greatest experience of my life."[41] Adrian Rogers and others said almost the same thing.[42]

It was a remarkable time, but what came next is difficult to fathom. The efforts of all that had gone before reached critical mass. A vision for spiritual awakening and the power of prayer found their focal point.

Bill Bright completed his first 40-day fast prior to the Orlando prayer meeting. Near the end of the fast, the Christian leader was reading 2 Chronicles and praying for revival. He believed God impressed upon his spirit a promise of a coming spiritual awakening to America. The specificity of the vision was remarkable: If two million believers in America would fast for 40 days, praying for revival, the year 2000 would be the beginning of spiritual awakening.[43]

My own life was indirectly impacted by Bright's challenge, even though I was initially unaware of his unusual vision or his 40-day fast. I was invited to preach at a large youth camp in Northwest Arkansas in the mid-1990s. The anointing on the camp was powerful. I was fasting that week when about 150 young people were saved and dozens surrendered to ministry. I have since met ministers in unexpected places all over the country who were among those who surrendered to ministry that week.

At the camp, one of the teaching sessions was led by Dr. Ronnie Floyd, who was pastor of a mega-church a few miles away. When he arrived that first morning, I was struck by how thin he looked. His testimony that day explained his gaunt appearance and much more.

Months earlier during his daily time with the Lord, unaware of Bill Bright's book, Floyd began to experience an impulse that he should fast for 40 days. The idea sounded bizarre to him, but the Spirit seemed to be leading in that way. During that season while he prayed through the serious implications of a 40-day fast, someone gave him Bright's book calling for people to fast and pray for revival.

Dr. Floyd took up the challenge. After the 40 days, a significant move of the Spirit occurred at his church. Since then, his church has more than tripled in size—often reaching more than 10,000 people every Sunday. God has used Floyd around the world, calling the church to fast, pray, and seek Him for revival. Dr. Floyd was speaking at the youth camp just a few days after his first 40-day fast had concluded. I was stunned by what he shared.

A few days later I called my friend John Yarbrough, then a pastor and leader in Georgia and a longtime prayer partner of mine. I told Yarbrough about Floyd's fast, the revival that broke out at his church, and the book by Bright.

About three weeks later, Yarbrough informed me that he was in day 17 of his 40-day fast! My call to him, Floyd's fast, and reading Bright's book had convinced him. He added one unwanted piece of information. He was adamant. God had shown him I was also to fast for 40 days. I was sure he had missed God on that, and I told him. But he was right. God made it unbearably clear to me that I was to fast and pray for 40 days. I obeyed the Lord—and 40 days without one bite of food, hours a day in prayer, and a relentless pursuit of God changed my life.

Around that time, it seemed to me as if every minister I knew was burdened for revival. The 20th century was coming to a close. People everywhere were fasting and praying. What we didn't know was that the prayer movement was just getting started. We were only drops in a stream. The rivers would flow in the 21st century. Spiritual awakening is coming.

THE ORGANIC PHASE (1999-PRESENT)

It's difficult to imagine two locations more different than Kansas City, Missouri—with its sweltering, muggy summers and windy, cold winters—and the tropical warmth and isolated views of the cliffs of Cape St. Vincent, Portugal. But in these two disparate locations, two young men, who had never met, were being prepared to prioritize the ministry of prayer and mobilize armies of prayer.

Mike Bickel was a pastor in Kansas City in the 1980s when he felt drawn by what he perceived to be unusual encounters with God. In time, he and a committed group of others, inspired by the Moravian prayer movement, launched a continuous prayer meeting that covered 13 hours every day. Four months later, on September 19, 1999, the group went full time with a 24-hour-a-day prayer meeting that has continued non-stop ever since.[44]

On the other side of the world, Pete Greig was camping on the cliffs of Cape St. Vincent in the 1980s. One night, he climbed out of his tent and started to pray. The cliffs are the most southwestern point of Portugal and therefore of Europe. With the sea crashing below, Greig (then a college student) prayed for the nations. As he prayed for Europe, he believes he saw a vision of an army of European young people worshipping the Lord.[45]

Years later, as a pastor frustrated with his own prayer life, Greig visited Herrnhut, in Germany, to learn about the Moravians and their 100-year prayer meeting. Inspired by what he learned, Greig led his own congregation in Chichester, England, to attempt something radical—a non-stop prayer vigil to operate 24 hours a day. To their surprise, people showed up and the 24/7 prayer movement was born.

The British pastor and his praying flock of young people didn't know Mike Bickle in Kansas City. They'd never heard of him, and it's certain Bickle had never heard of Greig. God led both men, however, to launch 24-hour prayer rooms in September 1999.[46] The prayer rooms from England have been reproduced into "an international, interdenominational movement of prayer, mission and justice; a non-stop prayer meeting that has continued for every minute of this century so far, in over half the countries on earth."[47]

WHAT'S HAPPENING?

Let me ask you some serious questions: What's going on? Has anything like this ever happened in modern times? Why are unceasing prayer movements erupting into existence?

In 2000, a South African businessman named Graham Power got a vision for a one-day prayer event for the purpose of repentance and to call upon God. A few months later, 45,000 people jammed into a rugby stadium in Cape Town to pray. The hunger of the people to do it again led to the formation of the Global Day of Prayer, reaching millions of people in more than 200 nations to join in prayer on Pentecost Sunday each year.[48]

In 2005, I was in Austin, Texas. I had never heard about any of these movements or that unceasing prayer was even *a thing.* I did know, however, what God was saying to me. I started leading my church to be a *house of prayer.* I didn't really know what it meant. I only knew I was led to press into prayer as never before. I was convinced the early Church prayed more than we do. So I preached on prayer, I organized prayer meetings, I wrote about prayer, I made pilgrimages with staff and large groups of church members to Brooklyn Tabernacle to learn—and we persisted through numerous challenges.

Somewhere around that time I began receiving emails from a pastor across town I didn't know named Trey Kent. He said he was leading a prayer ministry and wanted me to participate. At first I didn't, but things changed.

Before we move to the next chapter, let's circle back to Bill Bright. In 1995, he envisioned a spiritual awakening occurring before the end of the year 2000, involving radical repentance, fasting, and prayer.[49] Is the international prayer movement what he saw? Are we in the early stages of the next great awakening?

Chapter Seven

A PEOPLE OF PRAYER

By Trey Kent

One of the most unforgettable, powerful sermons I've ever heard is "Everything by Prayer" by A.W. Tozer. He took the phrase "everything by prayer" from the popular verse: "Do not be anxious about anything, but in *everything by prayer* and supplication with thanksgiving let your requests be made known to God. And the peace of God, which surpasses all understanding, will guard your hearts and your minds in Christ Jesus" (Phil. 4:6–7, italics added).

To be a people of prayer we must embrace not only the phrase "everything by prayer," but we must live a lifestyle fueled by unceasing prayer. I learned very early that unceasing prayer does not mean we never miss a minute or hour of prayer, but that we never quit praying. Unceasing prayer is unrelenting, persevering prayer as a lifestyle for the rest of our lives.

The story of Jesus and the two blind men from Matthew 20:30–34 powerfully illustrates unceasing personal prayer:

And behold, there were two blind men sitting by the road-

> side, and when they heard that Jesus was passing by, they cried out, "Lord, have mercy on us, Son of David!" The crowd rebuked them, telling them to be silent, but they cried out all the more, "Lord, have mercy on us, Son of David!" And stopping, Jesus called them and said, "What do you want me to do for you?" They said to him, "Lord, let our eyes be opened." And Jesus in pity touched their eyes, and immediately they recovered their sight and followed him.

We can draw four lessons from the desperate prayers of these two blind men.

LESSON ONE: CALL OUT TO JESUS

I believe unrelenting, unceasing prayer is driven by two unmistakable sources: our great need and God's empowering Spirit. These blind men were clearly needy, hurting, desperate, and burdened to cry out to Jesus. God is drawn to our weakness. True prayer emerges from our need for God and our need for help.

Most people are burdened by overwhelming needs. God made us needy. And He made us to pray. We can allow our needs to become our friends in prayer. Desperation keeps us calling out and seeking solutions. Needs ultimately drive us to God, who cares more than we do and knows how to answer our prayers in ways that give Him the most glory—and us the most good.

Like the two blind men, we must call out to Jesus. Human need may be a great instigator of prayer, but only the Spirit of God in us can enable us to pray without ceasing. He works in us so we won't quit praying! To become people of prayer, we must regularly be filled with the Spirit as Paul urges us in Ephesians 5:18. The Spirit of God is the Spirit of prayer. When our needs drive us to God, the Spirit keeps us coming back day after day, season after season, decade after decade. Paul teaches us that the Spirit helps us pray in our weakness (Rom. 8:26). And it's our weakness that makes way for the Holy Spirit to resource us in prayer.

One of my greatest questions—and one I am often asked—is, *what am I to pray about?* I can cry out about my needs, but that's not enough. *What else does Father God want me to talk to Him about?*

Jesus' answer to this question helps me immensely. The disciples asked Jesus to teach them to pray. Here's Jesus response in Matthew 6:9–13:

> "Pray then like this: 'Our Father in heaven, hallowed be your name. Your kingdom come, your will be done, on earth as it is in heaven. Give us this day our daily bread, and forgive us our debts, as we also have forgiven our debtors. And lead us not into temptation, but deliver us from evil.'"

The Lord's Prayer was given to teach us how to pray. These 52 words comprise the most important prayer guide you will ever follow. I build my daily prayer time in the morning around this model. As I seek to pray without ceasing throughout the day, I use this same model. The seven key themes are the basis for much of my prayer life. Remember, the 52-word prayer Jesus gave us contains the most important themes He wants to dialogue with you about.

Here are the seven themes from the Lord's Prayer that drive my prayer life:

- *Our Father*: connecting my heart as a son with the Father-heart of God.
- *Heaven*: focusing my heart and mind on my true home.
- *Holy Is Your Name*: exalting the name of the Lord as pre-eminent in all things.

- *Your Kingdom Come*: praying for the reign and rule of God in various life spheres.
- *Daily Provision*: asking God to meet physical, emotional, financial, relational, and spiritual needs.
- *Forgiveness*: receiving and giving forgiveness without limit.
- *Protection and Deliverance*: asking for protection from temptation and deliverance from evil.

I begin my day praying these themes. Often, I will not cover all seven themes during my morning prayer time. As the day progresses, I call out to the Lord and resume praying where I left off. It's been a very helpful model to bring a daily structure with great flexibility to my growing life of prayer. This is a guide but not the end.

In addition to the Lord's Prayer, there are many other things the Lord wants to talk with us about. Many of these come either from Scripture or from life's challenges and joys. Whether praying the Lord's Prayer, praying Scripture, bringing our needs and requests to God, or praying some other helpful model, the aim of our prayer focus must be to pursue a lifestyle of crying out to God.

LESSON TWO: CHALLENGES TO PRAYER WILL CONSTANTLY ARISE

The two blind men who cried out to Jesus were met with great opposition from the crowds in Jericho. The crowd rebuked them telling them to be silent (Matt. 20:31). That's how it works for us as well. Life, the devil, our fears, our circumstances, unanswered prayer, and sometimes well-meaning friends try to silence our cries to Jesus.

Far too often, we succomb to these temptations to stop praying. This is one of the chief reasons Jesus teaches us over and over to never stop praying, to keep on asking, seeking, and knocking—to be bold in our tenacious prayers for God to intervene with mercy.

I face three main temptations trying to silence my prayers:

- Temptation to think God is not hearing me
- Temptation to think it doesn't really matter if I keep praying
- Temptation to get too busy to pray.

Our church has faced several huge financial tests over the years. We cried out, fasted, prayed, and unified together. But for years we saw little movement. Then, in the most unexpected way, God answered our prayers. In one crisis, the landlord unexpectedly forgave our debt of more than $85,000! The next time we faced crisis, a new member surprisingly gave a $100,000 offering. God answers prayer!

This gives me hope today as I look back and see God's faithful hand on us. During the early years of the Unceasing Prayer Movement, I got very discouraged from the lack of buy-in from pastors and churches—and wondered if it really mattered if we kept mobilizing churches to pray. Here we are, 10 years later, and the prayers are making a significant impact on the heart of our city and beyond.

My biggest battle, even to this very day, is to refuse to let busyness in my heart, mind, and schedule choke out prayer. I keep reminding myself there is nothing more important I can do than pray. As S.D. Gordon said, "You can do more than pray after you have prayed, but you cannot do more than pray until you have prayed."

What about you? How is the enemy or your circumstances seeking to stop your prayers? I invite you to join me right now in praying a simple prayer: "Jesus, please help me to persevere in prayer and not quit."

There it is. I know He hears our sincere prayers and will help us today to be men and women of prayer.

LESSON THREE: LET THE CHALLENGES CAUSE YOU TO PRAY ALL THE MORE

The two blind men responded in a surprising way to the crowds yelling at them to be silent:

"But they cried out *all the more*, 'Lord, have mercy on us, Son of David'" (Matt. 20:31, italics added).

Are the challenges, lies, hardships, and voices trying to silence you actually causing you to cry out all the more? That's the work of the Spirit inside of us.

The Spirit prays without ceasing—and invites us to join His constant intercession. Paul urges us to pray "at all times in the Spirit, with all prayer and supplication" (Eph. 6:18). No human can pray without ceasing; the Spirit inside us does. We must join His cries.

Imagine the vast work the enemy stages to silence the prayers of God's people. Satan knows the power of our prayers. Samuel Chadwick, a great champion of prayer, taught: "Satan dreads nothing but prayer. His one concern is to keep the saints from praying. He fears nothing from prayerless studies, prayerless work, and prayerless religion. He laughs at our toil, he mocks our wisdom, but he trembles when we pray."

If this is true, we must devote our lives to praying God's prayers and walking in His will. Our great joy is to follow God and defeat the works of the enemy. Our cities are places that have been rampaged by Satan's schemes. The prayerless Church plays into the devil's ploys by refusing to stand against him in prayer. James 4:2 gives a clear rebuke to our prayerless ways: "You do not have, because you do not ask."

I wonder what our lives, families, neighborhoods, churches, and cities are missing that God would love to give, simply because we have been silenced by the barrage of Satan's schemes. This is the hour. We are the people to rise up and say, "No more!"

We are called to cry out in unity for God's Kingdom to come and His will to be done on earth as it is in heaven!

LESSON FOUR: JESUS CALLS TO THOSE CALLING OUT TO HIM

The astounding part of the story of the two blind men who kept calling out to Jesus, in spite of the great opposition, is that Jesus stopped and called out to them: "And stopping, Jesus called them and said, 'What do you want me to do for you? They said to him, 'Lord, let our eyes be opened.' And Jesus in pity touched their eyes, and immediately they recovered their sight and followed him" (Matt. 20:32–34).

Imagine with me today that because of our calling out to Jesus for Him to bring sweeping change to us and to our cities, Jesus calls out to us and says, "What do you want Me to do for you?"

That's an overwhelming thought. What do we want Jesus to do for us, for our families, for our cities, for our nation, and the world? For this, we must cry out in unceasing ways, in private and in public, until we see Jesus's mighty Kingdom overtake the kingdoms of the world! Jesus is inviting us to ask. He is calling out to us to call out to Him through prayer. He will hear our prayers, forgive our sins, and heal our land (2 Chron. 7:14).

One of the most strategic tricks of the enemy is to blind us to the power of prayer. Most Christians have no idea how prayer is viewed, honored, and celebrated in heaven. The only two things I know that interrupt the worship of heaven are when a sinner is saved and when prayer is brought before God. Both become a part of the grand celebration of worship and praise of all that God is and does. Do you realize how prayer is honored in heaven?

In Revelation chapters five and eight we see clearly that prayer rises like incense from God's people and is caught in heaven in golden bowls by angels and elders. It is then brought before the very throne of God. God obviously hears our prayers when we ask. He knows what we will say before we utter a word, but has chosen to have our treasured prayers caught in golden bowls by the inhabitants of heaven and brought physically before His throne!

Why? God honors prayer. Heaven knows the immense value of the prayers we pray. Hell knows the power of our intercession. It is only the Body of Christ that doesn't understand all that God does when we pray.

In Revelation 8:1–5, God receives the prayers of the saints before His fiery altar, and at the perfect time the answered prayers are thrown back to the earth. It's astounding to think about. This passage shows God ruling the end-time events by using the prayers of the saints as a part of the process. Let that sink in. God not only values our prayers, He uses them as a part of His governing of the earth.

John Piper shares these insights on this amazing passage in Revelation 8:

> The utterly astonishing thing about this text is that it portrays the prayers of the saints as the instrument God uses to usher in the end of the world with great divine judgments. It pictures the prayers of the saints accumulating on the altar before the throne of God until the appointed time when they are taken up like fire from the altar and thrown upon the earth to bring about the consummation of God's kingdom.
>
> In other words, what we have in this text is an explanation of what has happened to the millions upon millions of prayers over the last 2,000 years as the saints have cried out again and again, "Thy kingdom come . . . Thy kingdom come." Not one of these prayers, prayed in faith, has been ignored. Not one is lost or forgotten. Not one has been

> ineffectual or pointless. They have all been gathering on the altar before the throne of God.[50]

In Austin, a growing number of pastors and leaders see the urgency of raising up people of prayer and churches of prayer who never give up. This is vital to seeing both the awakening and the transformation we long to see in our city.

To be a people of prayer means we strive with the Spirit's power and with our brothers and sisters in Christ to pray without ceasing. We cry out to God; we use opposition as fuel for more prayer! We cry out *all the more.* We rejoice in a God who calls to us and asks what we want Him to do. We have been given the great privilege to be a people of prayer.

People of prayer are motivated, inspired, and empowered by the unfailing promises of God!

Chapter Eight

THE PROMISE OF PRAYER

By Trey Kent

God offers promises that will change your city! Not only does He promise that we can partake of His divine nature and escape the corruption of this world (2 Peter 1:4), but He also assures us that all His promises are *Yes* through Christ Jesus.

When we agree with God's promises (say, "Amen!") from both the Old and New Testaments, we can walk in confidence that Jesus died and rose again to do exceedingly abundantly beyond what we have seen or asked. He does this exceedingly abundant work through His praying Church (Eph. 3:20–21).

This assurance of fulfilled promises has changed my view of our city of Austin. Jesus died and rose again for way more than we've seen or experienced. So, I believe Jesus is delaying His return because He has an unfinished work to do in our cities. The path forward is through His great and precious promises that are ours in Christ.

Imagine if a mega-wealthy relative died and left you a huge inheritance that must be seized through the details of a 1,500-page document. To access all the benefits of this billion-dollar windfall, you must first know the document backwards and forwards. It's the same with the truth of God's Word. What promises has God given you for your city? You and other believers must do the detailed work of biblical study and prayer to discern promises you can claim over your city.

When I moved to Austin in 1993, I quickly saw some amazing strengths our city carries. We are the state capital of Texas and are known as the live-music capital of the world. We are home to one of the largest and most influential universities in America—the University of Texas. What can these natural strengths of the city mean for the Kingdom? What would Austin look like if she were transformed? We could be the live worship capital of the world! Austin would be a city of great spiritual influence—a leadership city for the Kingdom. As a transformed city, we could mobilize thousands upon thousands of young and old adults to take Christ to the nation and the world.

A BRIGHT FUTURE

What about your city? What natural or obvious gifts has God given to your city? What would these strengths look like if your city were transformed by Christ? Let these natural strengths be joined with the promises of God to cause you to pray for radical transformation for your city.

The great missionary and missionary mobilizer William Carey rightly proclaims, "The future is as bright as the promises of God." Apply this to your city. Your city's future is as bright as the promises of God. What you need is a group of men and women of God who will search out these great and precious promises and pray, unify, and work to see God's promises realized. This is the great and joyous work of the Church.

We have God's promises—and we know, "God is not a man, that he should lie, or a son of man, that he should change his mind. Has he said, and will he not do it? Or has he spoken, and will he not fulfill it?" (Num. 23:19). The best way to change a city is to pray and live God's promises as the source of your faith, hope, and love.

God has given us hundreds of precious promises to help guide our prayers and actions to see our city changed. These four promises guide me as I work with the citywide Body of Christ to see Austin transformed:

- My house shall be a house of prayer for all the nations (Mark 11:17).
- I will make your city a place of praise on the earth (Isa. 62:7).
- I will make Austin the light of the world, a city on a hill (Matt. 5:14).
- I will turn your spiritual desert into an oasis, even for the next generation (Isa. 44:3).

A HOUSE OF PRAYER FOR ALL NATIONS

Jesus dramatically cleansed the temple the final week of His life and said these words that still rock our city to this very day, "My house shall be a house of prayer for all the nations." Jesus called His Church a house of prayer. But He also calls each one of us a house of prayer because God's Spirit dwells within us (1 Cor. 3:16). When two or three gather in His name and agree, we are a united house of prayer (Matt. 18:19–20). Our heart cry is that Jesus will change greater Austin into a house of prayer for all nations.

Austin is the eleventh largest city in America. Our city has doubled in size during each of the last two decades. Now, more than 2.2 million people live in the greater Austin area—the five-county region. Recently, I read that three of the five counties—Williamson, Travis, and Hays—are exploding in growth. Every day, 120 people move into Williamson County, 120 move into Hays County, and 60 move into Travis County. That's 300 new people every day!

We are seeing an increase in people moving in from all nations, especially from Latin America, India, and Southeast Asia. I am thrilled Jesus is sending the nations to Austin! He is not sending them here to go to hell. He is sending them to our city because we live in the most prayed-for city in America. I believe all the prayers we have prayed over Austin will result in a massive evangelistic movement that will result in an unprecedented number of salvations. This is what it means to be a house of prayer for all nations.

I dream that our city will be filled with 24/7 houses of prayer north, south, east, and west—places of prayer and ministry always open to welcome people for all nations, backgrounds, and socio-economic situations and to share the love of Jesus with them. What if the entire city of Austin was transformed into a house of prayer for all nations? I am praying God will do this. Why not? Many Walmart stores and McDonalds are open 24/7. Are Walmart and McDonalds more important than the church?

The praying Church of greater Austin is the most important group of people that exists in our city. We have the most influence and have been given the powerful privilege of praying God's promises and working together to see our city transformed.

AUSTIN: A PLACE OF PRAISE UPON THE EARTH

God promises that when His praying Church gives Him no rest and takes no rest, He will make Jerusalem a praise upon the earth (Isa. 62:6–7)! God is describing a city where He is honored, the people are blessed, and widespread transformation takes place for His glory.

We've been claiming this promise over Austin for more than 10 years. Austin is our Jerusalem, and we are contending night and day for Jesus to make Austin a city of praise, a city exploding with worship of Jesus! Because we are affectionately called the live-music capital of the world, we are crying out for God to make us the live-worship capital of the world. It will take a miracle, but God's promises are given so we will believe Him in persistent prayer for nothing less than citywide transformation.

As we began crying out, we saw three unprecedented moves toward this end:

- Worship leaders began moving to Austin and worship schools were launched. A young generation has taken this live-worship capital prayer and is slowly turning it into a reality!
- A unity has developed among worship leaders across the city unlike any time in the last 25 years.
- A new generation of worship leaders is working together to lead citywide events, calling believers to worship God and see our city set on fire for Jesus. These new leaders are starting churches, taking worship into the streets, and working with seasoned pastors to bring an intergenerational unity to the city Church.

We must see by faith the end of our prayers! Unified worship is becoming more common in our city. It's a prelude to citywide houses of prayer and worship that will arise throughout our city, hosted and served by local churches partnering together. We know the best is yet to come!

A CITY ON A HILL

My wife, Mary Anne, and I recently returned from Israel. My favorite part of both trips I've made to the Holy Land is the Sea of Galilee. It's truly mesmerizing to see in person. To read the Gospels in light of this beautiful region is inspiring.

Our tour guide, Andre Moubarak, is a zealous Christ-follower born and raised in Jerusalem. As we toured the Sea of Galilee, he pointed out that in Jesus' day, the Roman cities across the lake from the Jewish areas would be lit up at night so that their light could be seen brightly from the northwest part of the sea. As Jesus spoke these words during the Sermon on the Mount, "You are the light of the world. A city set on a hill cannot be hidden" (Matt. 5:14), the thousands of listening Jews would immediately think of the powerful light show they saw as they gazed across the Sea of Galilee.

Our prayers in Austin—like yours for your city or region—are that our city will be a beacon of light and truth. We long for our radiance through Christ to shine forth for the world to see. We believe people will come from cities and nations to behold the work of God in our city. The University of Texas, located in the heart of Austin, has a saying that the city Church has adopted: "What starts here changes the world!" Poncho Lowder, pastor of Dreamers Church here in Austin, recently proclaimed, "What starts in prayer changes the world."

We believe that! Through unceasing prayer, we are becoming a city on a hill, the light of the world.

AN OASIS IN THE DESERT

Austin is a city that often transitions from drought to flood-stage rather quickly. After several years of Austin being covered in day-and-night prayer by area churches, I found this passage that I now claim for our current residents and for future generations: "For I will pour water on the thirsty land, and streams on the dry ground; I will pour my Spirit upon your offspring, and my blessing on your descendants" (Isa. 44:3).

Following a seven-year drought that almost consumed Lake Travis, our area water source, the Church in Austin began crying out for God to fill our one-third-filled lake and our one-third-filled lives. The lake levels are a barometer in our city for the state of the Church. For God to send floods on dry ground physically is an essential blessing, but we are laboring in prayer for something much greater! We believe God wants to flood our city with a modern day move of the Spirit that rocks old and young, black and white, rich and poor, Asian and Hispanic.

We are praying for an historic move of God that shakes the very foundation of our city and puts our city on the rock-solid foundation of Christ. We know this move of God will touch the young in our city. Austin's median age is 31 years old. Thousands are flocking to our city every week. The Church is praying day and night. We are sharing Christ. We are anticipating a mighty harvest of souls for Christ in the coming months and years. We must pray to this end and work toward this promise. We cry out and believe we will see floods of the Spirit setting things right in our city, bringing unprecedented unity, salvations, worship, prayer, and Christ-centered families and neighborhoods.

We know God wants you and your city Church to call out for "the more" that He has for you in the months and years ahead. The praying Church carries the most influence in your city—more than the city council, mayor, or school system. The praying Church is the key to a transformed city.

Please take the time now to ask God, "What are the promises from Your Word that You want us to pray over our city?" Begin asking key leaders and fellow believers what promises they have been given for your city. Collectively, begin crying out for God to fulfill those promises.

Chapter Nine

CITY OF PRAYER

By Trey Kent

As I write this chapter, we know of at least 25 cities in America and more around the world that have adopted or are in the process of adopting this simple monthly day of prayer for churches. Cities engaging with the America Prays strategy include: Bellingham, Federal Way, and Vancouver, Washington; Albuquerque, New Mexico; Austin, Dallas, San Antonio, San Marcos, and Houston, Texas; Tulsa, Oklahoma; Orlando, Florida; Little Rock and Fayetteville, Arkansas; Minneapolis/St. Paul, Minnesota; Grand Rapids, Michigan; Chico, California; Eugene, Oregon; Denver and Colorado Springs, Colorado; Providence, Rhode Island, and Hartford, Connecticut. The following nations are adopting this model we are calling World Prays: Mexico, Japan, Sri Lanka, Singapore, Malaysia, India, Argentina, and soon Canada.

We received reports recently that areas of Mexico are experiencing unprecedented blessings on their city since they launched 24/7. As I write this, we learned that 511 Indonesian cities gathered in united prayer for the harvest and for upcoming elections. Forty-four other cities around the world joined them in prayer. A total of 555 cities livestreamed together and nearly five million believers were united in prayer. The Indonesian prayer movement, possibly the largest in the world, has resulted in one Muslim turning to Christ every 15 seconds, according to a video produced by Muslims warning against the mass conversions to Christianity taking place in Indonesia. God is uniting cities around the world to join the global cry for a great awakening!

Significant prayer movements are also springing up in Nashville, Tennessee, where 400 churches have mobilized 40,000 believers to pray for every person in the city by name. Kansas City, Missouri, has hosted day-and-night prayer at International House of Prayer since 1999. Cincinnati, Ohio; Wichita, Kansas; Sacramento, California; Reno, Nevada; Washington, D.C.; New York, New York; and many more cities have growing citywide prayer movements. This is just the tip of the iceberg. The prayer movement is and will continue to impact cities through local churches praying together in unity.

The Church was born in a prayer meeting. Armin Gesswein, the founder and former director of Revival Prayer Fellowship, said, "When Jesus went back to heaven, all He left behind was a prayer meeting." That 10-day prayer meeting in the upper room in Jerusalem has changed everything forever for the Church. It's noteworthy that God is raising up once again this rhythm of day-and-night prayer that overflows into powerful city transformation. This is God's strategy to change cities through His praying Church.

Citywide prayer movements are being launched by Brian Alarid and the America Prays team, as well as by names and faces we may never know. Alarid not only leads America Prays, he is also running point in Albuquerque, leading an excellent New Mexico Prays team that is seeing astounding results in that city and the state of New Mexico.

Jason Hubbard is also a team member on the America Prays team and leads Washington Prays and the Whatcom County prayer movement centered in Bellingham, Washington. In this chapter, I feature these two outstanding stories to show the power of prayer in transforming a city.

WHATCOM COUNTY STORY

Hubbard launched 24/7 prayer in the Bellingham area of Whatcom County in 2009. They originally called it the One Church Initiative, but now refer to it as Day2Pray (in partnership with America Prays, Washington Prays, and Light of the World Prayer Center). Whatcom County and Austin, Texas, both launched the same prayer strategy on the same day (January 1, 2009) without knowing the other existed. God is amazing!

Hubbard, though a young man, is known as the grandfather of this movement and has been instrumental in launching this one-church-a-day prayer model in cities throughout America. He has also been an influential mentor to those desiring to see their city changed through united prayer.

Hubbard provided this inspiring report on all God has been doing in Bellingham and Whatcom County:

> About 10 years ago the churches of Whatcom County (population: 200,000) launched a united prayer strategy to cover the area in 24/7 prayer. Each church adopts a day of prayer once a month, every month, and asks their people to commit to 30- or 60-minute segments of prayer during their church's Day2Pray. Forty-six local churches are now committed, led by their pastors, and each local church appoints a prayer coordinator to oversee its day of prayer. Also, teams of Kingdom-minded believers representing nine different sectors

of culture gather on a regular basis to help provide prayer points for transformation: arts and media, business, church, development/social services, education, family, government, health care, and international missions. This canopy of united, strategic, and sustainable prayer has led to remarkable transformation over the last ten years.

- Ten thousand new believers baptized in water in the churches of Whatcom County.
- Eighty church plants in ten years.
- Fifteen hundred new Hispanic believers in last few years and eleven new Hispanic churches planted.
- Abortion numbers have dropped significantly since 2007; numbers have been cut in half in a university town since the prayer strategy was launched.
- En Gedi, a thriving ministry helping women come out of sex trafficking and exploitation, reported a 90 percent rate of women coming to Christ and transitioning into healthy lifestyles.
- Christian schools have come together in unity after years of division.
- Adoptions have been increasing (children into Christian families) and Skookum Kids, a robust foster care ministry, has launched.
- United Pastors prayer group meets consistently for prayer representing 70 percent of the pastors in the area.
- Light of the World Prayer Center, a citywide house of prayer, began in 2008 and now has 40 corporate prayer meetings each week.
- A Christ-awakening is erupting on our college campus, with ten percent of student body meeting weekly among seven campus ministries. Several of our Christian professors

are united together in the Western Christian Faculty.

- Project 92, an effective missions ministry to the least-reached peoples in the world, has launched. In 2018, 5,500 people came to Christ (1,500 were baptized in water) in areas of North India, Bhutan, Bangladesh, and Nepal. These are first-generation believers in areas with virtually no access to the gospel.

Our vision is to see a God-breathed Christ awakening movement erupt in the Northwest! We are praying day and night for Christ to have His supremacy in every area of culture in Whatcom County to the Glory of God the Father (Col. 1:18). In the paraphrased words of the Moravians, "May the Lamb who was slain receive the due reward for his sufferings in Whatcom County and beyond" (Rev. 5:12).

This is a link to a 13-minute video that describes the prayer strategy and highlights a few transformation stories: *lowpc.org.whatcomstory.*

ALBUQUERQUE STORY

I met Brian Alarid, pastor of Passion Church, Albuquerque, New Mexico, and founder of America Prays, when we were working together on the Decision American event the Billy Graham Evangelistic Association (BGEA) held in capital cities across America. Brian was the regional manager for the BGEA team overseeing their work in 10 states. As Brian heard about Unceasing Prayer in Austin, he felt God prompting him to launch the same in Albuquerque, throughout the state of New Mexico, and eventually across the United States. We partnered to launch New Mexico Prays in January 2017, and since then unprecedented miracles are occurring in New Mexico—with the bull's-eye focused on Albuquerque. New Mexico Prays now has more than 100 churches that have adopted a day of prayer. It is beginning to transform the state, especially Albuquerque.

Here's Brian's firsthand testimony:

> Adopting a day of prayer is not the end game, but it is a simple way for churches to make prayer a part of their monthly rhythm and develop a culture of prayer. "God has used New Mexico Prays to not only bring the Body of Christ together throughout our state in focused prayer, but also our congregation at New Beginnings Church," says Richard Mansfield, senior pastor of New Beginnings Church, Albuquerque.
>
> Unceasing prayer is happening in homes, places of work, college dorms, coffee shops, parks, and churches. Through united prayer, we are witnessing Jesus transform our economy and confront the abortion crisis. The hungry are being fed and the poor are being served. We took Jeremiah 29:7 to heart and began praying for the peace and prosperity of our state: "Also, seek the peace and prosperity of the city to which I have carried you into exile. Pray to the Lord for it, because if it prospers, you too will prosper." God makes it clear that prayer plays a vital role in the safety and prosperity of your community.
>
> New Mexico ranked a last-place 50th in the family prosperity index, 49th in economy, and had the second highest poverty rate in the nation. But when God's people pray, God hears from heaven and things begin to change. A state that was facing an expected $200 million deficit has a $1.2 billion surplus. According to Bloomberg news report, since the beginning of 2017, New Mexico is number one in job increases and wage increases. To be clear, new econom-

ic policies, thriving oil and gas industry and the hard work of many have made this possible. However, it is too drastic a turnaround to be explained by natural solutions alone.

Another area where we have seen answers to prayer is in the abortion issue. Albuquerque, the largest city in New Mexico, has been known as the "late-term abortion capital of America." Since churches began praying 24/7 for an end to late-term abortion in New Mexico, three abortion clinics have closed. Furthermore, for over two decades the University of New Mexico's Health and Sciences Department conducted research on aborted baby parts. In a remarkable turn of events, UNM ended the controversial program.

Church unity is one of our main prayer focuses, in accordance with Jesus' prayer in John 17:21: "that they may all be one, just as you, Father, are in me, and I in you, that they also may be in us, so that the world may believe that you have sent me." A unified Church is the most credible witness to the world that Jesus is Lord. We have asked God to unite the churches of New Mexico across denominational lines, and Jesus has begun to answer that prayer. Southern Baptist, Reformed, Presbyterian, Calvary Chapel, Pentecostal, Charismatic, Catholics, Messianic Jews, and non-denominational churches have come together in prayer to see God transform our state. We have laid aside our theological differences to exalt the name of Jesus Christ.

We believe that only a united Church can heal a divided nation. "I have been in Albuquerque for 38 years and I've never seen pastors come together for anything like this. It is changing the climate," says New Mexico Ministry Network Pastor Michael Dickenson.

New Mexico Prays churches are uniting to serve our communities and love them like they have never been loved before. On June 23, 2018, more than 100 churches, nonprofits, businesses, and government agencies partnered to sponsor a Convoy of Hope outreach at the Albuquerque Convention Center. We gave away more than $1 million worth of goods and services—including 80,000 pounds of groceries, 9,900 meals, 1,600 gardens in a bag, and 3,000 pairs of shoes. Now we are partnering with Albuquerque public schools to feed more than 2,000 needy and homeless children and their families for Thanksgiving. As in the days of the Moravians, prayer is moving us to mission and service.

On October 7, 2017, we launched America Prays to unite and equip 40,000 churches in prayer for a national spiritual awakening. This is a Jesus-centered, local-church-based prayer movement that God is using to transform communities. Imagine what will happen when every city, county, and state in America is covered in worship-saturated prayer!

CITYWIDE PRAYER/OUTREACH STRATEGY

As churches throughout the nation are adopting monthly days of prayer, we ask churches to unite by praying toward a common seven-point prayer focus. Pastors and prayer coordinators can obviously create their own prayer guides, but we believe there is power in uniting the praying Church citywide, countywide, statewide, and nationwide.

Here are the seven major prayer focuses of America Prays:

- Pray for Unbelievers to Be Saved. Pray that people's hearts will be opened to repent of their sins and confess Jesus as

Savior. Pray that every person in the world will be able to hear the gospel and the Word of God in their native language (Matt. 9:37–38, 24:14; Rom. 10:1; 2 Peter 3:9; Acts 26:18).

- Pray for a National Spiritual Awakening. Pray that Jesus will revive the Church and awaken our nation to His greatness and supremacy. Pray that God will pour out His Spirit on America, forgive our sin, and heal our land. Pray that millions of Americans will be convicted by the Holy Spirit, repent of their sins, and turn to God with all their hearts (2 Chron. 7:14; Dan. 9:18–19; Ps. 85:6; Hab. 3:2; Acts 2:37–41).
- Pray for Unity between Pastors and Churches. Pray that denominational, theological, and ethnic walls will come down so that pastors will love each other, pray together, and serve each other (John 17:20–23; Ps. 133:1; Eph. 4:3–6).
- Pray for Families. Pray that Jesus will heal, restore, and strengthen every marriage and family. Pray that husbands will love their wives like Christ loves the Church and that wives will respect and submit to their husbands. Pray that the hearts of parents will be turned toward their children to love them and raise them in a God-honoring way. Pray that children will respect and obey their parents (Gen. 2:24; Josh. 24:15; Ps. 127:3–5; Mal. 4:6; Eph. 5:22-33, 6:1–4).
- Pray for Racial Reconciliation. Pray that God will heal our nation of racism and that God will use the Church to stand against racial conflict, violence, and prejudice. The Church must lead the way in racial reconciliation by modeling love and respect for every person regardless of the color of their skin or their ethnic background (Rom. 10:12–13, Gal. 3:28, Acts 10:28, 34–35, John 7:24, 1 John 2:9, James 2:9, Rev. 7:9).

- Pray for Life to Be Valued and Protected through All Stages of Life, Beginning at Conception. Pray for God to break the culture of death in America and restore a culture of life. Pray for legalized abortion to come to an end (Ps. 139:13–16; Jer. 1:5; Prov. 24:11; Deut. 21:8–9).
- Pray for Local and National Government Leaders. Pray that God will give them wisdom to make wise decisions and to govern with integrity, justice, and mercy (1 Tim. 2:1–2; Rom. 13:1; 1 Peter 2:17; Titus 3:1–2; Micah 6:8).

Once the basic prayer strategy of 31 or more churches adopting a day of prayer in the city takes root, the churches can begin to mobilize teams to pray and work toward God's miraculous intervention in one of the seven main areas. As area prayer meetings are organized, these themes can be a key focus of the prayers. Recently hundreds gathered from dozens of churches in Austin, Texas, at Hyde Park Baptist Church to pray for the first prayer point (Pray for Unbelievers to Be Saved) and later another gathering focused on point seven (Pray for Local and National Government Leaders).

The dream is that teams will emerge to focus on working out these prayers into practical steps and connect with those inside and outside the "church-world" to see our cities changed for God's glory. This was in God's heart when He inspired Jeremiah to write: "But seek the welfare of the city where I have sent you into exile, and pray to the Lord on its behalf, for in its welfare you will find your welfare" (Jer. 29:7).

How will you launch or join 24/7 prayer in your city?

Chapter Ten

LAUNCHING 24/7 PRAYER IN YOUR CITY

By Trey Kent

God is raising up catalysts to help launch 24/7, unceasing prayer in churches and cities across America. Brian Alarid (founder and director of America Prays) and I just returned from an amazing trip to Arkansas to talk to pastors and leaders about launching the America Prays strategy in that state. In northwest Arkansas, Dennis Peterson, director of the Fayetteville Prayer Room, is ignited with vision and is now working to mobilize 100 churches in the region to adopt a monthly day of prayer! Logan Bloom, founder of Arkansas for Christ and the leader of Arkansas Prays, is also set to mobilize churches in the central Arkansas region, targeting Little Rock and beyond. God has given Bloom great favor and trust among area pastors to begin this movement of 24/7 prayer. Prayer champions like these are springing up in towns and cities across America.

Maybe God is raising you up. Perhaps you know of a person in your city, county, or region who needs to know more about America Prays and how he or she can join efforts to mobilize churches in prayer. This amazing work of God is happening through normal people like you and me—people upon whom God has placed His hand in this hour to see the unprecedented global prayer movement take root in your city.

LAUNCH A DAY OF PRAYER

The process of launching 24/7 unceasing prayer in the greater Austin area began in 2008 as our local church, Northwest Fellowship, adopted a day of prayer every month. We originally hoped other churches would join us, but we were determined pray for our city, regardless, because we believe this is God's call upon us. We started by asking folks within our church to adopt one hour of prayer on the fourth Monday of every month.

It worked! Twenty-four people signed up. When they had to miss, we asked others to fill in. In this initial phase of launching a day of prayer, we asked each person to pray for one hour and then "pass the baton" by calling the next person on the list and pray for him or her at the start of each new hour.

STEPS TO LAUNCH A DAY OF PRAYER

Here are some simple steps you can take to launch prayer in your city, even if you are the only church in the beginning:

- Step 1: Pastor selects a half or full day for the church to pray every month.
- Step 2: Pastor appoints a prayer coordinator to manage the

day of prayer and volunteers.

- Step 3: Pastor shares the vision with the church on a Sunday morning a few weeks before the first day of prayer.
- Step 4: Church members sign up to pray for 30–60 minutes on the chosen day of prayer.
- Step 5: Coordinator sends reminders to volunteers as they pray from home, work, school, or church. (For more specifics, see *AmericaPrays.org*.)

As our day of prayer took root with two or more people adopting each hour, a greater prayer culture also took root at Northwest Fellowship. We worked strategically to grow our prayer culture each year and add as many new people as possible. In our fourth year of Unceasing Prayer, we took the next step of inviting our church members to pray at church in our prayer room. Although it was not required, we believed it to be another step in deepening our prayer commitment. For the past seven years, on the fourth Monday of every month, our church and prayer room are open for 24 straight hours and filled with praying believers crying out in twos or threes for a mighty move of God in the greater Austin area.

There's always that first step for your church. If you are the senior pastor, work with your staff and prayer coordinator to launch a day of prayer each month to intercede for your city. If you are a staff member or involved in your church, talk to your pastor about setting up a monthly day of prayer. Your first step can begin the simple journey of changing your church and city through united prayer.

CAST VISION TO OTHER CHURCHES

I am certain either God has already started a prayer movement in your city—or He wants to begin one now. Once you've established one 24-hour day of prayer in your local church, bring together pastors in the city and invite them to adopt a day of prayer in their churches. As we approached our 24/7 prayer launch in January 2009, we hosted vision meetings for pastors in October, November, and December 2008. After these three citywide lunches and many one-on-one meetings, we finally filled our 31 days of prayer.

In some cities around the country, the process has been longer. In fact, it's a marathon. Refuse to compare. Unceasing prayer is needed until Jesus returns, so don't lose heart if it takes a while to get it launched. I thought for years that our movement wasn't taking root fast enough. Now, as I look back over the 10 years of day-and-night prayer in Austin, I see the momentum increasing every year!

Since launching 24/7 prayer in 2009, our yearly strategy is to invite every pastor we know to attend an Unceasing Prayer luncheon in the fall, usually in late October. At this lunch, we cast vision for the next year of unceasing prayer. We ask churches to sign up for the first time, while urging those already committed to renew their commitment for the coming year. This yearly lunch highlights the vital importance of 24/7 prayer in our city.

We also highlight key leaders in our city, such as Tim Hawks, pastor of Hill Country Bible Church—one of our early adopters in the Unceasing Prayer Movement. Hawks and his church have planted more than 30 churches in the Austin area. He now is a senior leader of the national board of Christ Together, an organization empowering cities across the earth to take responsibility to reach every man, woman, and child with the gospel of Jesus Christ. We work together to see our city covered in 24/7 prayer and the gospel shared citywide. We celebrate what God is doing in greater Austin and equip our praying pastors and leaders toward the next year of 24/7 prayer.

Unceasing Prayer is spreading in greater Austin. The area cities of Round Rock and San Marcos are beginning to launch their own versions of the prayer movement. San Antonio, Texas, has launched unceasing prayer. The Dallas-Fort Worth area (DFW Prays) has the vision of mobilizing 500 churches in 30 quadrants to pray 24/7 for spiritual awakening. They've already mobilized 200 churches to adopt a day of prayer.

We see a growing hunger in cities across the earth to unite in 24/7 prayer for spiritual awakening. Desperation is increasing as human solutions prove ineffective for long-term transformation.

BUILD A TEAM OF PASTORS TO LEAD

One of the biggest challenges in our city's recent history—the drying up of our area lake and water source—caused us to call a citywide prayer meeting. This resulted in the expansion of our Unceasing Prayer Team from three pastor-leaders to seven. God uses challenges for our good and His glory.

Our team has a goal of meeting monthly for lunch, prayer, planning, and building relationships. All these elements are vital for our team to stay unified and working together to see the movement of prayer grow in greater Austin.

I recommend these essential qualities in choosing pastors to serve on the citywide prayer movement team:

- They are proven unifiers.
- They are committed to prayer in their local church.
- They are excited about working as a team without being the hero or focal point.
- They are willing to adjust their schedules and their church's schedule for team meetings and citywide prayer events.
- They can help mobilize other pastors to build cultures of prayer.

Nothing is as important as building a strong leadership team. In your city, think about the obvious pastors who can help lead a movement of prayer for decades to come. Invite them to pray with you about forming a team to see your city covered in 24/7 prayer. Imagine, you get to be a part of launching a movement of prayer that will make history in your city!

It's a new day for you, your team, and your city when 24/7 prayer emerges. One word of caution for choosing leadership for your city: we discovered it's vital to find a pastor who feels called to lead this team, someone with a burning passion for 24/7 prayer. Cities with this kind of pastoral point leadership have flourished, where other cities have not.

FOLLOW GOD'S VISION FOR YOUR CITY

As we see city movements of prayer emerge across the United States, we see great diversity in the ways God is moving. Please understand there is no cookie-cutter approach to launching, growing, and sustaining a citywide prayer movement. Follow God's leadership in your city.

For example, Albuquerque, New Mexico, focuses on partnerships with the city government. Bellingham, Washington, mobilizes teams to work in areas of business, arts, education, etc. In Austin, we focus on growing the prayer movement through citywide prayer meetings, pastors' prayer gatherings, launching new movements in regional areas, and by partnering with existing ministries that already lead well in areas of education, evangelism, and business.

Comparison is terrible. It ruins our joy. C.S. Lewis claimed that all comparison is rooted in destructive pride. Celebrating the uniqueness of your city, the uniqueness of the growing prayer movement, and the unique partnerships you will forge with the gifted ministries and people in your city is essential to seeing your city transformed.

DON'T EVER QUIT

Unceasing prayer doesn't mean you never miss a minute or an hour or a day. Unceasing prayer means you never quit praying! Jesus promises speedy justice to those who cry out to Him day and night: "And will not God give justice to his elect, who cry to him day and night?" (Luke 18:7). Jesus begins this parable urging us not to lose heart: "And he told them a parable to the effect that they ought always to pray and not lose heart" (Luke 18:1).

We must persevere in citywide, church-based, pastor-led, 24/7 prayer day and night until Jesus returns. We must not lose heart or quit, because God will hear and He will bring speedy justice to our cities in response to the prayers of His praying Church.

Chapter Eleven

RESULTS OF PRAYER

By Kie Bowman

It isn't often you hear about a prayer meeting on the evening news, especially in Austin, Texas. However, in 2014, when the city gathered to pray for rain at the height of a drought, local media outlets paid attention. Admittedly, at times they appeared skeptical and seemed to report with a thinly disguised "tongue in cheek" about religious leaders gathering to pray for rain. Nevertheless, we planned a prayer meeting for rain—and local television news decided to cover it. Their reporting, regardless of the motive, helped get the word out to a much larger audience that the citywide prayer meeting was happening.

The need was real enough. We were experiencing the worst drought in Austin's history, and the demand for water had never been greater due to an unprecedented lack of rainfall and the taxing needs of a rapidly expanding population. Explanations of the seriousness of the water shortage sounded more like exaggerations, but it was truly that bad.

Austin's drought was the worst on record and spurred lawmakers to consider multiple options, none of which promised rain.[51] The main water source for our fast-growing city is taken from Lake Travis, fed by the Colorado River. During the worst days of the drought, we experienced months with virtually no rain and daily temperatures higher than 100 degrees for most of the summer. It was an economic and human crisis with no good options. The computer models showed worsening conditions, more severe water restrictions, and no rain in the forecast.

One morning, a group of pastors and intercessors from the prayer movement gathered at 6 a.m. to pray at a local church, as they routinely did. This particular morning, they were at Hyde Park Baptist Church. After they had prayed for a couple of hours, one of the intercessors announced she sensed an impression from the Lord that we needed to call a citywide prayer meeting for rain. Another prayer warrior chimed in to report he had received the same impression while he was praying. Everyone agreed the prayer meeting should be held at Hyde Park Baptist Church.

A month later, 1,000 believers from numerous churches gathered to pray and worship. For almost two hours, we asked God for rain. We needed more than a little. Lake Travis is full at 681 feet (surface elevation), and it had dropped to less than 618 feet. Lake Travis is almost 19,000 acres in size, so to increase the depth of the lake one acre foot requires 325,851 gallons of water. The lake level was down in an unprecedented amount, and the water needed to fill Lake Travis was mind-boggling (more than 20 million gallons needed)! So, 1,000 people gathered to pray for a miracle. We prayed for rain.

That next weekend torrential rains and flash floods covered Austin. It was only the beginning. Ignoring every computer model predicting more drought, the rains fell regularly and relentlessly. The lake started to fill up. The prayer for rain and the sudden downfall was covered by a national news outlet.[52] The unseasonably heavy rains continued regularly for months. It wasn't uncommon for someone to jokingly chide me with a comment like, "Pastor, could you pray it stops now?"

We watched God answer prayer with a modern-day nature miracle. In less than two years, the millions of gallons of water needed to fill Lake Travis pushed the levels back to 681 feet. God answered our prayers in one of the most conspicuous ways imaginable.

UNITY AMONG BELIEVERS

In addition to answered prayer that ended a drought, there are other results of the prayer movement in greater Austin. One of the most obvious is the unity of the Body of Christ. One of the easiest ways to evaluate this unity in Austin is to ask some of the city's Christian leaders.

Tim Hawks has been in Austin for 30 years. He is the lead pastor of Hill Country Bible Church, one of the largest and most mission-minded churches in the United States. Today, thousands of worshippers gather at Hill Country Bible every week in one of its multiple locations. In addition, Hawks is a leader in the national Christ Together Network[53] I suspect no one in Austin understands the religious demographics and spiritual dynamics of our city better than Tim Hawks.

Recently, I asked Hawks to reflect on the impact of the prayer movement in Austin. His thoughts were insightful. He remembers coming to Austin three decades ago to a "divided" city. Churches within the same denomination were battling each other at times. Denominations were contentious. The "charismatic/non-charismatic conflict was raging" and churches were going to "war" with an increasingly secular city—rather than praying for and ministering to the city in Jesus's name.

Today's climate is different. Churches work together. The city leaders now believe the churches bring value to Austin. Pastor Hawks remembers Austin Mayor Steve Adler recently saying when he came to office it was with the idea that government's role is to improve people's lives, with help from the faith community. Now he believes the faith community improves people's lives and government is alongside to help! That's a significant change. Hawks believes prayer helped move the dial.

In addition, Hawks sees pastors working together with greater unity. He believes the prayer movement, along with the efforts of ministries like Christ Together, has brought about that change. The prayer movement has "raised awareness of the value of the 'Big C' Church in Austin."[54]

I agree with Tim Hawks. In Austin, mega-church pastors and church planters stand side-by-side in prayer and vision for the city. Bible church pastors, Baptist pastors, Charismatic pastors, Hispanic pastors, Asian pastors, Black pastors, traditional church pastors, contemporary church pastors, baby boomer pastors, and millennial pastors all pray, worship, and work together to share Christ with our city and cover the city in 24/7 prayer. That kind of unity doesn't just happen by accident. People prayed for that result, and we never stop praying to maintain and improve it.

RACIAL FELLOWSHIP

The Emanuel African Methodist Episcopal Church in Charleston, South Carolina, is the oldest African Methodist Episcopal (AME) church in the south. On Wednesday, June 17, 2015, a few congregants gathered with the pastor for prayer. A white stranger entered the church and was warmly welcomed by the black Christians who enjoyed praying together. The night ended in terrible violence when the young, white stranger opened fire, killing nine innocent Christians while they lovingly sat in their church praying. It was a national tragedy.

One week later, hundreds of people, mostly white, joined with the Metropolitan AME Church in Austin to pray, pledge our love for our brothers and sisters, and share in their grief. One of the leaders of the Unceasing Prayer Movement, Rick Randall, had a relationship with Jordan Mkwanazi, pastor of the Metropolitan AME Church. Pastor Mkwanazi is a distinguished, Christian gentleman originally from Zimbabwe. He has a gentle pastor's heart for his congregation and a fierce zeal for the spiritual growth of other people. Pastor Mkwanazi greeted and welcomed us as brothers as we crowded into his church's worship center until we had to move many to overflow rooms. It was a significant night of prayer. The leaders of the Unceasing Prayer Movement put a stake in the ground, declaring our repudiation of racism and our love for every child of God regardless of race.

I wonder if many communities could rally a prayer meeting of hundreds of people from multiple churches to gather in a church of a predominantly different race within one week of a tragedy. I believe it came together because the infrastructure for the prayer movement was already in place. The relationships already existed. Our movement isn't about traditional, bureaucratic structures requiring multiple levels of decision approvals. It's a movement with alacrity and flexibility tied together by a common love for Christ and a burning passion to pray and lead others to pray. Imagine how quickly cities could respond to tragedies if the pastors of every city were already praying together. Imagine how much more quickly revival could come!

One of my joys that night at Metropolitan AME Church was meeting Pastor Mkwanazi. We hit it off with him right away, and he has become a part of our seven-person leadership team. His passion to build a culture of prayer in his church is obvious.

In addition to Mkwanazi's leadership, we intentionally reach out to other pastors from African-American, Hispanic, and Asian congregations. We include them in leadership in both the decision-making process and publicly as prayer leaders in our prayer gatherings. Men like Daryl Horton, Abraham Perez, Gerald Johnson, DeChard Freeman, John Monger, Charlie Lujan, Kevin Workman, Sylvester Patton, A.W. Mays, and many others represent different races and ethnicities, but we are brothers in prayer. We eat meals together, preach in each other's churches, attend each other's church events, and pray together. We may not be able to end racism, but we can stand against it and pray against it. One of the results of the prayer movement is greater fellowship among the various racial groups in our city.

The result of greater friendship among God's family from different races is more than just good fellowship. Our larger vision is mobilizing every church to grow in prayer. Pastor Mkwanazi is a prime example. After the prayer meeting at his church, we became fast friends, and he has since mobilized his historic church toward even more prayer. He recently shared this insight:

> Following one of America's greatest tragedies in church history (nine people having Bible study and prayer at The Emmanuel AME Church in Charleston, South Carolina, gunned down by a white supremacist on June 17, 2015), I received a phone call from the Unceasing Prayer Movement of Austin, Texas, with a gracious offer to gather and call the churches of Austin in prayer at my church—Metropolitan AME Church. Hundreds gathered (black, white, Hispanic, Asians) in prayer and remembrance. Little did I know that I was being exposed and introduced to one of the most powerful and significant prayer movements in any American city.

I have since been invited to be a part of this extraordinary prayer movement, led by seven committed and dedicated brothers whose passion for prayer is unrelenting and unquenchable. My first and foremost impression was the discipline of prayer that was exhibited through these brothers in their local churches. It became obvious to me as I listened to their testimonies during our monthly meetings that prayer was an integral part of their local ministries. They were not just talking prayer; they had, in fact, built a culture of prayer in their respective ministries. I have been a pastor for over 32 years in three respective leading cities in Texas, and I have never encountered a group of pastors/ministers whose passion, dedication, and focus is praying for their city.

Undoubtedly, the Unceasing Prayer Movement has played a major role in my own focus and commitment to prayer as a pastor of a local church in Austin. Like most churches I know of, prayer has always been a part and parcel of our local ministry. Metropolitan AME Church was traditionally committed to our Wednesday night prayer meetings, as are many churches. Being part of the Unceasing Prayer Movement quickly brought to my realization a rude awakening that there is a difference between having Wednesday night prayer meeting and developing a culture of prayer. The New Testament Church "all joined together constantly in prayer" (Acts 2:42), suggesting a mindset that places prayer at the heart of a church's activity—always a part of everything the church does.

This new revelation about developing a culture of prayer challenged my willingness to take a traditional church that only had a few people meeting on Wednesday night for a prayer meeting to developing a culture of prayer. How to

> do that was the impending question. I quickly realized this was not going to be an overnight undertaking. The change and the desired outcome were only going to happen based on several conditions: (1) As a pastor, I had to take the lead; (2) I had to make the culture of prayer mandate a part of my vision, and (3) I had to remember this was going to be a process.
>
> In the last two years, Metropolitan AME Church has shifted toward becoming a church that embraces a culture of prayer. We have moved from Wednesday night prayer meetings to overnight prayer gatherings to having every Monday morning intercessory prayer. Prayer has become the center stage of our ministry. We are evolving as a church into fearless, bold, and committed prayer warriors.[55]

Pastor Mkwanazi's zeal speaks volumes. His own church's commitment to developing a culture of prayer can work in any church. Prayer is contagious!

THE PRAYER MEETINGS

If the average mid-week gathering in most churches is the standard for a prayer meeting, then we are doomed. Most people don't even attend prayer meetings. John Franklin states the problem in his book *And the Place was Shaken*: "... by and large we have abandoned meaningful prayer meetings. Most that remain are anemic and weak."[56] Fortunately, in Austin the energy around our prayer meetings is anything but average.

After the citywide prayer meeting for rain, the Unceasing Prayer Movement caught a fresh vision of the city in prayer. Since that event, we have coordinated citywide prayer meetings at least once per quarter.

Our lowest-attended gathering has been 150 people. Our best attendance was 2,000. We average between 300 and 500 people at a typical gathering. Most importantly, we have never had a disappointing prayer meeting. They are all accompanied with power. They are a highlight of my life. I love our prayer meetings.

A few years ago, the Southern Baptists of Texas decided they wanted to host mid-day prayer meetings for pastors throughout the state of Texas. The state was subdivided into 18 regions, and my friend Ted Elmore, a leader in evangelism and prayer for Baptists, helped coordinate the events. Most of the regional events were not well attended. I told Ted about the Unceasing Prayer Movement and asked permission to let our mixed denomination leadership team help coordinate the event in Austin—and he agreed. While the average attendance throughout Texas for the prayer meetings was about 13 pastors, the prayer meeting in Austin was attended by 300 people at ten o'clock in the morning!

A few weeks later, Dr. Jim Richards, the executive director of the Southern Baptists of Texas Convention, asked if our prayer team could help lead a segment of their upcoming annual meeting held in Austin that year. Of course I agreed, and we worked with Ted Elmore to host a 24-hour, nonstop prayer room in the lead up to the prayer meeting. We reached out to Malachi O'Brien, a national prayer leader from Kansas City, to help us coordinate the logistics. When the time came, we had 24 worship teams leading one-hour segments of worship and a dedicated room for non-stop prayer at Great Hills Baptist Church, where my friend Danny Forshee serves as pastor. Several people stayed in the prayer room almost the entire time.

When the time for the prayer meeting arrived, at least 1,500 people were present. Our Unceasing Prayer Movement team led the prayer time, joined by our honorary member Malachi O'Brien. It was electric. Jim Richards tweeted it was the greatest prayer meeting he had ever been in. We have led numerous prayer meetings with hundreds of people and where the power of God's presence is manifestly conspicuous. They are a major force in deepening the resolve for prayer in the Body of Christ in Austin.

When we recapture the New Testament vision of prayer meetings, spiritual awakening won't be far behind. Prayer meetings change the world!

AMERICA PRAYS LAUNCH

Another result of the prayer movement in Austin is the growth of the movement in other places. It seems prayer begets prayer.

Brian Alarid is a young leader with an unusually engaging personality. Alarid was working with the Franklin Graham team to coordinate Graham's prayer rallies at the state capitals around the United States in the run-up to the 2016 presidential election. Alarid was responsible for Texas and the other southwestern states. He and Trey Kent became friends while they worked together to coordinate the rally at the Texas capitol in Austin.

Alarid has a deeply devoted heart for prayer and almost immediately recognized the power of the Austin Unceasing Prayer Movement model. God stirred his heart with the possibilities. After praying and fasting, he launched New Mexico Prays and then America Prays. The stated goal of America Prays is to involve 40,000 churches in 24/7 prayer. His model for this ambitious vision is the model he learned from Trey Kent in Austin. As of this writing, America Prays has launched in 14 states and continues to expand.

YOUNG LEADERS ENGAGED

Another result of the prayer movement is the involvement of millennials. Young leaders like Kyle Hubbart, who leads a day and night prayer room in the west Austin community of Lakeway, echoes what other leaders have noticed: Austin's Christian community is unified. In Hubbart's words, "We don't just tolerate each other, we actually like each other."

In his enthusiasm for the prayer movement, he likens what he sees to something akin to the experiences in the Book of Acts. Unified efforts at street evangelism often grow directly out of one of our citywide prayer gatherings. Leading a prayer room can be both rewarding and draining, but the larger prayer movement in the city and the frequent prayer gatherings have often provided Hubbart the encouragement needed to continue through challenges.

Blaise Raccuglia, a gifted worship leader and soloist and once a contestant on *The Voice*, is, like Hubbart, in his early 20s and attends our prayer gatherings regularly. John David Vasquez directs a school of worship in Austin and lives to pray and lead worship. We often call on Vasquez and Raccuglia to form a band and lead worship at one of our events. When we operated the 24-hour prayer room at the Southern Baptists of Texas Convention, Vasquez arranged to cover the entire time with worship leaders who contributed their talent without charge.

Recently, Will Davis, Jr., a member of the Unceasing Prayer leadership team, pastor of the large multi-site Austin Christian Fellowship, and well-known author, pressed the rest of the team to include the younger leaders from around the city in our ministry. We always involve younger leaders on the teams who lead in prayer at citywide prayer gatherings. But we wanted to go farther, so we invited a select group of young ministers with a heart for prayer to attend our monthly leadership meeting. In addition, recently we scheduled two hours at the H.O.P.E. Prayer Room (House of Prayer East) for a time of worship and prayer for the "young guns" and our existing leadership team. These young men and women are branching out on their own to lead prayer and worship gatherings all around our city with incredible passion.

RESULTS POINT TO HOPE

In one sense, prayer is its own reward, since we are talking to God. Spending time with Him and leading others to do so is satisfying in and of itself—even if we see no other results.

The results we see, however, are pointing toward something else that is sure to come. Numerous leaders in the city sense an unusual unity and a growing passion for prayer. A younger generation of prayer leaders is emerging. Every spiritual awakening has been preceded by a prayer movement, and it is clear we are in a swelling prayer movement now. We can only conclude that a powerful spiritual awakening is in our future.

So, until we begin to reap that harvest, we will persist in unceasing prayer. We invite you to join us by submitting to what God wants you to do in your city!

ENDNOTES

CHAPTER ONE

1. "The Largest Earthquakes in the United States," *infoplease.com/world/earthquakes/largest earthquakes-united-state*. Accessed March 19, 2019.

CHAPTER TWO

2. Rick Duncan, "3 Ways to Beat the Monday Morning Ministry Blues," *pastors.com/beat-monday-blues/*. Accessed March 18, 2019.
3. John R. W. Stott, "The Message of Acts," *The Bible Speaks Today* (Downer Grove, IL: InterVarsity Press), 121.
4. Fred A. Hartley III, *Everything By Prayer* (Camp Hill, PA: Christian Publications, Inc., 1984), 12.

CHAPTER FIVE

5. Jim Cymbala, *Fresh Wind, Fresh Fire: What Happens When God's Spirit Invades the Hearts of His People* (Grand Rapids, MI: Zondervan, 1997), 71.
6. "Nikolaus von Zinzendorf: Christ-centered Moravian 'Brother,'"

Christianity Today, *christianitytoday.com/history/people/denominationalfounders/nikolaus-von-zinzendorf.html.* Accessed March 28, 2019.

7. "Why It's a Good Idea to Pray," Christian Teaching Resources, *christianteaching.org.uk/whyitsagoodideatopray.html.* Accessed March 28, 2019.
8. "A Prayer Meeting that Lasted 100 Years," *Christianity Today*, *christianitytoday.com/history/issues/issue-1/prayer-meeting-that-lasted-100-years.html.* Accessed March 28, 2019.
9. "Christian History Timeline: The World of 1732," The Christian History Institute, *christianhistoryinstitute.org/magazine/article/the-world-of-1732.* Accessed March 31, 2019.
10. Thomas S. Kidd, *The Great Awakening: The Roots of Evangelical Christianity in Colonial America* (New Haven & London: Yale University Press, 2007), 9.
11. "The Moravian Founding of Nazareth, Pennsylvania, *This Month in Moravian History*, Issue 91, May 2015 (Bethlehem, PA: Moravian Archives), *moravianchurcharchives.org/this-month/15_05%20Nazareth.pdf.*
12. "John Wesley; English Clergyman," *Encyclopedia Britannica*, *britannica.com/biography/John-Wesley.* Accessed March 30, 2019.
13. Todd C. Ream, Jerry Pattengale, and Christopher J. Deavers, editors, *The State of the Evangelical Mind: Reflections on the Past, Prospects for the future* (Downers Grove, IL: InterVarsity Press, 2018), 44-45.
14. Robert O. Bakke, *The Power of Extraordinary Prayer* (Wheaton, IL: Crossway Books, 2000), 88-89.
15. J. Edwin Orr, *The Fervent Prayer: The Worldwide Impact of the Great Awakening of 1858* (Chicago, IL: Moody Press, 1974), 1.
16. Ibid., 4.
17. Ibid., 4.

18. Roy J. Fish, *When Heaven Touched Earth: The Awakening of 1858 and Its Effects on Baptists* (Azle, TX: Need of the Times Publishers, 1996), 33-34.
19. Robert O. Bakke, *The Power of Extraordinary Prayer* (Wheaton, IL: Crossway Books, 2000), 113.
20. Ibid., 112.
21. Ibid., 115.
22. Roy J. Fish, *When Heaven Touched Earth: The Awakening of 1858 and Its Effects on Baptists* (Azle, TX: Need of the Times Publishers, 1996), 34.
23. Ibid., 34.
24. J. Edwin Orr, *The Fervent Prayer: The Worldwide Impact of the Great Awakening of 1858* (Chicago, IL: Moody Press, 1974), 5.
25. J. Edwin Orr, *The Flaming Tongue: The Impact of 20th Century Revivals* (Chicago, IL: Moody Press, 1973), 17.
26. Richard M. Riss, *A Survey of 20th-Century Revival Movements in North America* (Peabody, MA: Hendrickson Publishers, Inc., 1988), 41.
27. "Evan Roberts Testimony—1878-1951," The Revival Library, *revival-library.org/index.php/pensketches-menu/evangelical-revivalists/roberts-evan-his-own-testimony*. Accessed March 29, 2019.

Chapter Six

28. Richard M. Riss, *A Survey of 20th-Century Revival Movements in North America* (Peabody, MA: Hendrickson Publishers, Inc., 1988), 42.
29. "The Jesus Revolution, June 21, 1971," *Time, content.time.com/time/covers/0,16641,19710621,00.html.* Accessed April 16, 2019.
30. Larry Eskridge, "'Jesus People' – a movement born from the 'Summer of Love,'" *The Conversation, theconversation.com/jesus-people-a-movement-born-from-the-summer-of-love-82421.*

Accessed April 15, 2019.

31. "Revivals," Asbury University, *asbury.edu/academics/resources/library/archives/history/revivals/*. Accessed April 16, 2019.
32. Peter Wagner, *Prayer Shield* (Ventura, CA: Regal Books, 1982), 13.
33. "History," National Day of Prayer, *nationaldayofprayer.org/history*. Accessed April 16, 2019.
34. "Dick Eastman," Every Home for Christ, *ehc.org/dick-eastman*. Accessed April 16, 2019.
35. "History," National Day of Prayer, *nationaldayofprayer.org/history*. Accessed April 16, 2019.
36. "Dick Eastman," Every Home for Christ, *ehc.org/dick-eastman*. Accessed April 16, 2019.
37. Elmer L. Towns, Daniel Henderson, *The Church That Prays Together: Inside the Prayer Life of 10 Dynamic Churches* (Colorado Springs, CO: NavPress, 2008), 27-29.
38. Mac Pier, "How to Pray for Your City," September 9, 2013, *Christianity Today, christianitytoday.com/thisisourcity/newyork/how-to-pray-for-your-city.html.*
39. Bill Bright, *America's Call to Fast, Pray, and "Seek God's Face,"* (Orlando, FL: NewLife Publications, 1995), 19.
40. Ibid., 19.
41. Ibid., 22.
42. Ibid., 20.
43. Ibid., 29.
44. "A History of the Prayer Movement," International House of Prayer Kansas City, *ihopkc.org/about/*.
45. Pete Greig, *Dirty Glory* (Carol Stream, IL: NavPress/Tyndale House 2016), 10.
46. Alex Malaska, "A Brief History of 24-7 Prayer," Worship And The Word, *worshipandtheword.com/a-brief-history-of-24-7-*

prayer/. Accessed April 17, 2019.

47. 24-7 Pray.com, *24-7prayer.com/about*. Accessed April 17, 2019.
48. "About," Global Day of Prayer, *globaldayofprayer.com/about/*. Accessed April 16, 2019.
49. Bill Bright, *America's Call to Fast, Pray, and "Seek God's Face"* (Orlando, FL: NewLife Publications, 1995), 29.

Chapter Seven

50. John Piper, "The Prayers of the Saints and the End of the World," January 9, 1994, Desiring God, *desiringgod.org/messages/the-prayers-of-the-saints-and-the-end-of-the-world*. Accessed June 6, 2019.

Chapter Eleven

51. Brent Walton, "Central Texas Drought Is Worst on Record," Circle of Blue: Where Water Speaks, *circleofblue.org/2015/world/central-texas-drought-worst-record/*. Accessed April 23, 2019.
52. "The Blaze," May 29, 2014, *theblaze.com/news/2014/05/29/heres-what-happened-after-christians-begged-god-to-bring-rain-to-water-starved-texas-city*.
52. Ed Stetzer, "What Is Christ Together Network and How Does It Work to Saturate a City?" *Christianity Today, christianitytoday.com/edstetzer/2017/may/christ-together-network.html*. Accessed April 23, 2017.
54. Author's personal interview with Tim Hawks, March 26, 2019.
55. Author's personal interview with Jordan Mkwanazi, April 19, 2019.
56. John Franklin, *And the Place Was Shaken* (Nashville: Broadman & Holman Publishers, 2005), 20-21.

ABOUT THE AUTHORS

Pastor Trey Kent planted Northwest Fellowship in 1993 and has been in full-time ministry since 1986. He has a Master of Divinity from Oral Roberts University and did Doctor of Ministry work at Fuller Seminary. His passions are Jesus, prayer and his family.

He is the blessed husband of Mary Anne, the grateful father of daughters, Lindsay, Christina, and son-in-law, Nick Gamez, and the proud grandfather of Samuel David.

In 2009, God led Trey to launch the Unceasing Prayer Movement mobilizing more than 100 churches to pray 24/7 for unity and revival in Austin, Texas, where it has continued for 11 years and counting!

Trey also wrote *Revival Cry: Contending for Transformation in this Generation.*

Dr. J. Kie Bowman has served as senior pastor of Hyde Park Baptist Church in Austin, Texas, since 1997. He speaks throughout the United States and internationally in numerous evangelism and pastors' conferences each year, including recently preaching keynote sermons at the Southern Baptist Convention, and at the National Day of Prayer National Leadership Summit. He has been a keynote speaker for The International Baptist Convention in Interlaken, Switzerland, and presented a paper on American Evangelicalism at The Oxford Roundtable at The University of Oxford, England, as well as preaching in Paraguay, England, and at the First Baptist Church of Bethlehem, Israel.

Dr. Bowman holds a Doctor of Ministry from Southwestern Baptist Theological Seminary where he also serves as a trustee. He continues to hold numerous denominational leadership positions, including president of the Southern Baptists of Texas Convention. Dr. Bowman has authored five books and contributed to about a dozen others.

Together with other local leaders, Dr. Bowman gives leadership to the Unceasing Prayer Movement in Austin, Texas.

Kie has been married to Tina since 1981. Tina and Kie have three adult children, Amanda, Laura, and Joseph.

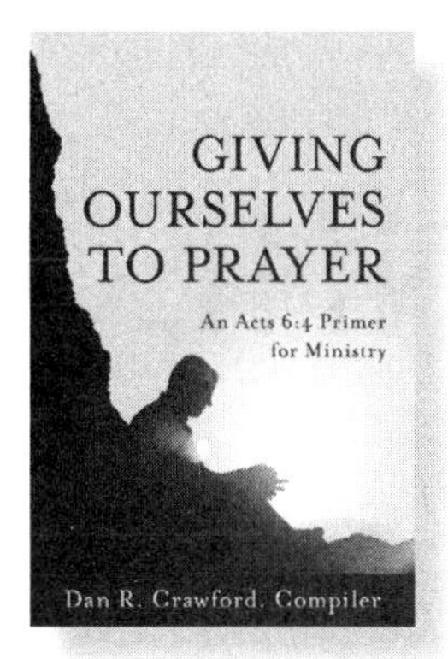

Giving Ourselves to Prayer

An 80-chapter, 584-page book written by professors, pastors and prayer leaders, that covers 4 sections: "The Theological Foundation of Prayer," "The Personal Passion for Prayer," "The Corporate Expression of Prayer," and "The Global Impact of Prayer."

52 Creative Ways to Pray

A resource loaded with ideas to liven up your personal prayer life, small group prayer, and larger prayer gatherings.

Pray the Word for Your Church

Includes 31 Scripture-based prayers to pray over a church. Teaches the user both to pray God's Word and to pray God's purposes in the life of a church.

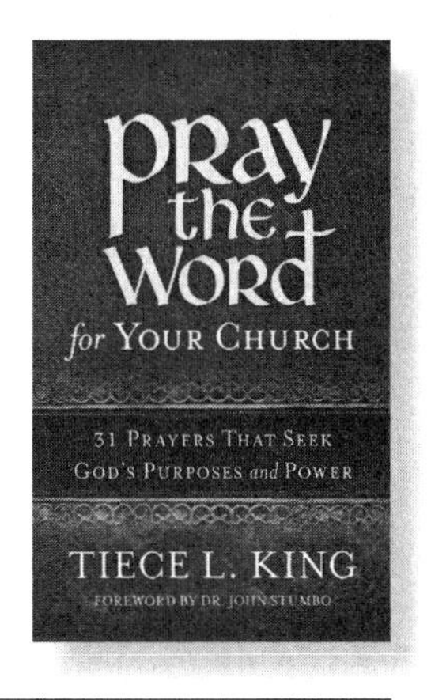

Targeted Prayers for Your Church

A scripture-based prayer guide with 31 prayers that focus on God's blessing in the different ministries in a local church.

prayershop.org